CENTRALLY PLANNED CHANGE

CENTRALLY PLANNED CHANGE

A REEXAMINATION OF
THEORY AND EXPERIENCE

Robert Mayer
Robert Moroney
Robert Morris

with contributions by: *Robert Barre*
John W. Dyckman
Robert A. Gordon
Benjamin Pasamanick
Anthony Pascal
Thomas Plaut
Allan Schick
Melvin M. Webber

UNIVERSITY OF
ILLINOIS PRESS

Urbana Chicago London

LIBRARY OF CONGRESS CATALOGING IN PUBLICATION DATA

Main entry under title:

Centrally planned change.

Proceedings of a conference, sponsored by Brandeis University and University of North Carolina, which was the 2d of 2 related conferences; proceedings of the 1st conference are entered under: Morris, Robert, 1910– ed. Centrally planned change; prospects and concepts.

1. Social policy—Congresses. 2. United States—Social policy—Congresses. 3. Social change—Congresses. I. Mayer, Robert R., ed. II. Moroney, Robert, 1936– ed. III. Morris, Robert, 1910– ed. IV. Brandeis University, Waltham, Mass. V. North Carolina. University.

HN65.C45   309.2'12   74-8240
ISBN 0-252-00435-3

PREFACE

In the early 1960s a spirit of social and scientific adventure spread in the United States overcoming the weariness which followed World War II. The belief grew that productive ingenuity now made possible the creation of a society in which material want could be abolished. The social and behavioral sciences, along with economics, produced fresh insights into the processes of social change in industrial society. Together these insights led to renewed confidence that scientific methods could be applied to the solution of problems of society and theoretically designed plans for improved government could be drawn up. Belief in the "Great Society" prevailed.

At the beginning of that period a conference was held at Brandeis University on the theme, "Centrally Planned Change: Prospects and Concepts," which brought together sociologists, political scientists, social welfare educators, and planners. That conference sought to elaborate on the theoretical underpinnings of what was then called planning to improve the social welfare in order to help service organizations take part in the great events in the making.[1]

[1] See Robert Morris, ed., *Centrally Planned Change: Prospects and Concepts* (New York: National Association of Social Workers, 1964). This publication was supported by the

The atmosphere in 1970 was much less heady. Poverty, deviance, violence, and tension among social groups remained unabated and in some cases increased despite the vast appropriations by government for many kinds of service programs. Skepticism among some social scientists about the feasibility or desirability of massive centralized planning by government to improve social conditions emerged. Community control and grass-roots participation became popular again. In government, the public administrators and professionals of the past decade began to be replaced by businessmen and management specialists less committed to social improvement than to short-term benefit-cost efficiency.

In 1972, Brandeis University and the University of North Carolina organized a second conference to reexamine the subject of centrally planned change. The thirty-two participants were more diverse than in 1963, representing economists, city planners, political scientists, public administrators, budget and management administrators, and health planners, as well as social workers and social planners.[2] The purpose of the meeting was to bring together in the present-day mood of pessimism and discouragement those who had taken part in large-scale government planning efforts to determine if this mood was justified, and if not, what could be salvaged from the past and what new ideas held hope for the future. Was it possible to talk of central planning by government that would not only manage but also prevent the occurrence of large-scale social problems? This review differed from that of 1963 not only in the type of participants involved, but also in the broader definition given to the term welfare—it encompassed not only the provision of social services but the management of the economy and of the urban environment as well.

The conference was organized around a few commissioned

National Association of Social Workers and the Morris and Bertha Treuhaft Memorial Fund.

[2] The names of participants in the conference are listed in the appendix together with their fields of interest.

papers which sought to summarize the American experience in governmental planning in three fields (mental health, employment, and urban development) in order to provide an empirical foundation for a discussion of planning theory. Other commissioned papers dealt with specific theoretical questions. Most of the conference was spent in dialogues among the participants about the key questions posed by these papers. The intent of the meeting was to ascertain whether agreement existed among planners about basic principles, and to lay out the lines for further theory building about planning for human welfare which could be subjected to empirical testing.

The text follows the basic structure of the conference only insofar as it deals with the same descriptive and theoretical subjects. A conference of this sort, even if it follows a tightly structured format, is full of bypaths, repetitions, and discontinuities. The authors have used the recorded discussions, the cases, and the papers to prepare a coherent treatment of the subjects considered in three days of intensive discussion. The recorded discussions among participants for the most part have been woven into the text, along with the commissioned papers, to present a more succinct treatment of each topic. Chapter 8 reproduces in its entirety (with only necessary editorial changes) the discourse of the final conference session.

The authors are aware of the dangers in attempting such a synthesis of views, especially for a relatively new field in which the ambiguities of language and of subject matter are so great. However, the search for rational and scientific means which can be linked to democratic political processes to allow government to deal constructively with fundamental problems of social distress and disorder must continue. If the theories and methods of planning for human welfare are unclear and incomplete, there remains the hope that further systematic work will reduce these flaws. The Employment Act of 1946 initiated a period of economic planning with neither clear tools nor with full agreement about theories of intervention in the economy. But twenty-five years of sustained work through the Council of viii *Centrally Planned Change*

Economic Advisors has led to significant advances in both theory and methodology. The answers regarding social planning may not be developed for a very long time. The intentions of the organizers of the Quail Roost Conference and of this volume will be realized if some semantic underbrush has been cleared away, if a few areas of agreement among planners have been identified, and if questions for the next stage of study and analysis have been more sharply defined.

Acknowledgments

This book is the product of many contributors whose names appear throughout the volume. The Morris and Bertha Treuhaft Memorial Fund and the Center for Studies of Metropolitan Problems of the National Institute of Mental Health provided generous financial support for this conference. William Treuhaft and Henry Zucker of Cleveland, John Parker, Head of the Department of City and Regional Planning, University of North Carolina, and Arnold Gurin, Dean of the Florence Heller Graduate School for Advanced Studies in Social Welfare, Brandeis University, gave continuous encouragement throughout. Ted Droettboom, John Oliver, Ken Daly, and Howard Sumka were responsible for the conference recording and provided critiques which were very useful in the preparation of this volume. Barbara Isaacson and Shirley Ritter provided invaluable secretarial service, and Lou Ann Brower contributed a clear editorial style.

CONTENTS

1 A Reexamination of Centrally Planned Change   1

2 Three American Efforts at Centrally Planned Change   17

3 Some Alternate Views of Centrally Planned Change   78

4 Consensus and Control   100

5 Planning within a Decentralized Framework   111

6 The Use of Market Mechanisms in Centralized Planning   135

7 The Technology of Planning   158

8 Machiavelli and Cellini: A Dialogue on Central Planning   178

9 Perspectives and Prospects   205

Appendix   221

Index   224

Acronyms Used in Text

CAB   Civil Aeronautics Board
CAMPS   Coordinated Area Manpower Planning System
CEA   Council of Economic Advisors
FCC   Federal Communications Commission
FHA   Federal Housing Administration
JOBS   Job Opportunities for Better Skills
ICC   Interstate Commerce Commission
NASA   National Aeronautics and Space Administration
NIMH   National Institute of Mental Health
NLRB   National Labor Relations Board
OMB   Office of Management and Budget
ORD   Office of Research and Development
PERT   Program Evaluation and Review Technique
PPB   Program Planning and Budgeting
PPBS   Program Planning and Budgeting System
WIN   Work Incentive Program

CHAPTER ONE

A REEXAMINATION OF CENTRALLY PLANNED CHANGE

The crises and changes that characterized the 1960s forced a growing awareness among Americans of critical social needs that were national in scope and required national solutions. The federal government responded in a variety of ways, which resulted in considerable experimentation in public intervention.

Yet none of these efforts constitutes national planning or centrally planned change as treated in this book. The War on Poverty, the various amendments to housing legislation, the Community Mental Health Centers Act, the Manpower Development and Training Act, and the Model Cities program were attempts by the federal government to attack problems through initiatives taken at the local level.[1] The Civil Rights Act, Medicare, and the Supreme Court decisions regarding school desegregation involved solutions requiring initiatives on the part of the federal government but lacked the necessary tools for implementation. These approaches have been criticized as merely *ad hoc* reactions to a long-standing vacuum in our social arrangements for meeting national needs. The persistence of serious social problems—crime, urban decay, pollution, racial inequality, poverty, and unemployment—after several years of these programs suggests the critics have their point.

[1] Roland Warren, *The Community in America* (2nd ed.; Chicago, Ill.: Rand McNally, 1972), p. 360.

The experience with governmental intervention which characterized the 1960s suggests the need for clarifying the meaning of centrally planned change. Each word in the phrase reflects an aspect of a unique process, the attempt to effect *change* in the society through programs *planned* by the *central* government. While the phrase is susceptible to interpretation along many dimensions, which may range from the administration of a service program to the degree of control over society exercised by a totalitarian government, for purposes of this book, centrally planned change [2] is defined as,

1. Public efforts which are *national in scope*, that is, which take into consideration the needs of the *entire population* with respect to some aspect of human need;
2. The assignment of *authority* and *control* over resources to specific public structures to achieve stated goals;
3. A *developmental process* which provides continuous guidance or management over time to one major system in society;
4. The precipitation of *redistributive effects*, that is, actions which change or alter resource allocations.

The requirement "national in scope" implies inclusiveness of population affected and not necessarily comprehensiveness of effect.[3] Centralized planning takes into consideration the needs of the entire population with respect to a given goal, that is, adequate medical care for all and not just a selected segment of the population such as "the indigent" or the aged, or those living in specific geographical areas. Centrally planned change dif-

---

[2] Various components in this working definition are found in the writings of James Q. Wilson, John Friedmann, Amitai Etzioni, Y. Dror, and many others.

[3] This distinction is similar to that of "universal versus selective" in Richard M. Titmuss, *Essays on the Welfare State* (London: Allen and Unwin, 1958); and "institutional versus residual" as discussed by Harold L. Wilensky and Charles N. Lebeaux, *Industrial Society and Social Welfare* (New York: Russell Sage Foundation, 1958), p. 138.

fers in this way from tentative or limited target programs often called demonstration programs or "innovative planning." [4]

Control over resources is tempered in our democratic society by some form of participation by the citizenry or its elected legislative body. While conceptually, centrally planned change suggests a high degree of autonomy with respect to the selection of goals, it is inconceivable to us in a democratic society that any planning body would be allowed to select these goals completely divorced from some degree of ratification by the citizenry. Our definition assumes that basic goals are arrived at by some consensus-making body such as a legislature, but that considerable discretion is delegated to a planning body to select within those broadly stated goals more specific, time-bound objectives.

Centrally planned change is seen as developmental in that continuous guidance is provided over time through "megapolicies" or broad policy guidelines.[5] Such planning is distinct from more time-limited program planning that addresses a particular problem. The latter, sometimes referred to as adaptive planning [6] or disjointed incrementalism,[7] posits objectives on the basis of departures from present practice.

And finally, centralized planning, as we see it, is capable of achieving change with respect to some characteristic of a system, such as income distribution. It is distinguished from system maintenance or "the registering of an equilibrium among contending interest groups." [8]

[4] John Friedmann, "A Conceptual Model for the Analysis of Planning Behavior," *Administrative Science Quarterly*, 12 (September, 1967), pp. 225–252.
[5] Yehezkel Dror, "Planning in the United States—Some Reactions of a Foreign Observer," *Public Administration Review*, 31 (May–June, 1971), p. 399.
[6] Friedmann, "A Conceptual Model for the Analysis of Planning Behavior."
[7] Charles E. Lindblom, *The Policy-Making Process* (Englewood Cliffs, N.J.: Prentice-Hall, 1968).
[8] James Q. Wilson, "An Overview of Theories of Planned Change," *Centrally Planned Change*, ed. Robert Morris (New York: National Association of Social Workers, 1964), pp. 12–29.

4 *Centrally Planned Change*

The character of centrally planned change can be further delineated by contrasting it with the dominant style of American planning, "interest group liberalism" or incrementalism. Interest group liberalism rests on the assumption of pluralism as the basic nature of American public policy. It has been characterized as a continual contest among "interest group leaders" who represent potential or organized support from voters.[9] T. J. Lowi[10] notes three essential deficiencies in such an approach to public policy: (1) incrementalism, (2) undermining of popular control, and (3) lack of protection for unorganized interests.

Incrementalism refers to the tendency of pluralistic decision-making to produce "departures from the past," an inherently conservative public policy. The end result of interest group liberalism is policy that is agreeable to existing vested interests. Any changes which do occur are likely to be disjointed—they may add up to a desired change in the state of affairs over time, but more likely they will be at cross purposes. There is little basis in pluralism for proposing radical or dramatic changes in system variables.[11]

A second deficiency in interest group liberalism is the tendency to reduce all issues to the aggregate of private group interests and to delegate authority for policy formulation and execution to special interest groups. As a result, public responsibility for guidance is abdicated and mechanisms for popular accountability of policy execution are emasculated.

And last, pluralism or interest group liberalism is criticized because of its failure to protect the interests of unorganized groups or permanent minorities. Indeed it has been suggested that the prevalence of this form of societal guidance perpetuated racial injustice prior to the civil rights movement and kept the poor and consumers virtually dependent on industrial and commercial establishments which are more organized.

[9] Lindblom, *The Policy-Making Process.*
[10] Theodore J. Lowi, *The End of Liberalism* (New York: Norton, 1969).
[11] Charles E. Lindblom, *The Intelligence of Democracy* (New York: Free Press, 1965).

Dror, a major proponent for rational planning, takes a different tack in criticizing incremental planning.[12] Recognizing that a rapid change in values and goals of social action renders comprehensive plans or master designs impractical, he argues that suboptimization will invariably result in doing the wrong things more efficiently. What is needed is not incremental planning, but "megapolicies to maximize options and multi-use resources that can meet unforeseen goals and values rather than be directed at operational targets." [13]

This study of centrally planned change does not deal with the comparison of governmental versus private corporate planning. Furthermore it does not describe a single model of central planning applicable for all sectors. Rather, we are focusing on planning within the governmental sphere and on the issues and requirements common to all substantive areas of planning, whether mental health, employment, or urban development.

Our definition of centrally planned change and its elaboration will serve as the form of this book. The concepts on which it is based will be examined from multiple perspectives and in the light of real world experience to see whether a firm conceptual foundation exists for central planning in America.

ISSUES IN CENTRALLY PLANNED CHANGE

The central issues arising from the concept of centrally planned change are (1) the amount of control to be exercised by centralized authority in providing the necessary direction for society, and (2) the achievement of consensus on the part of members of society about the directions or goals to be pursued.[14]

An inherent conflict is generated by these two requirements. Attempts at controlling or directing any social group, no matter

[12] Yehezkel Dror, "Muddling Through—Science or Inertia," *Public Administration Review*, 24 (September, 1964), pp. 154–157.

[13] Yehezkel Dror, "Planning in the United States," p. 399.

[14] This discussion is based on the central thesis put forth by Amitai Etzioni in *The Active Society* (New York: Free Press, 1968).

how well intentioned, have a tendency to decrease the level of legitimacy granted centralized authority or the amount of consensus in the group.[15] Not everyone values with equal strength the goals or directions pursued, and any given course of action is likely to benefit some more than others, as those who question the validity of the concept "the public interest" remind us.[16] This inherent tendency of societal guidance to generate dissensus requires that control efforts be modified or accompanied by efforts to broaden consensus among members of the group.

Consensus demands that goals and directions be broadly representative. The process of consensus-building involves providing opportunities for newly formed and neglected groups to increase their influence while overrepresented groups decline in influence. This process limits the control exercised by centralized authority. A preoccupation with achieving a balance among the interests articulated by competing constituencies compromises the freedom of centralized authority to chart new directions. Thus an emphasis on consensus-building can weaken the very control function it is supposed to strengthen.

Given a pluralistic society such as ours, faced with a "multiplicity of societal perspectives . . . which cannot be integrated into a single . . . hierarchy of values," [17] is any degree of consensus possible? These differing perspectives usually are resolved through negotiation and bargaining.[18] Where can we

[15] This same position is taken by Gouldner in his criticism of Parson's view of system change; Alvin W. Gouldner, *The Coming Crisis of Western Sociology* (New York: Basic Books, 1971).

[16] Lindblom, *The Policy-Making Process.*

[17] John Friedmann, "The Future of Comprehensive Urban Planning: A Critique," *Public Administration Review*, 31 (May–June, 1971), p. 317.

[18] This is basically the position of Edward Banfield, *Political Influence* (Glencoe, Ill.: Free Press, 1961); Martin Myerson and Edward Banfield, *Politics, Planning and the Public Interest* (Glencoe, Ill.: Free Press, 1955); James Thompson and Arthur Tuden, "Strategies, Structures and Processes of Organizational Decisions," *Comprehensive Studies in Administration*, ed. James Thompson (Pittsburgh, Pa.: University of Pittsburgh Press, 1959), pp. 195–213.

find or how can we build the consensus on social purposes necessary to centrally planned change?

Proposed Alternatives to Centrally Planned Change

Given the double-edged nature of centrally planned change—active citizen input but ineffective central control, or active but unresponsive central authority—many say centralized planning is not possible in the American context. Some form of less centralized control is proposed. Two alternatives have been selected for close examination here. One is the movement for local community control of basic institutions and the other is the proposed use of market mechanisms in lieu of centralized bureaucracies for the delivery of public services.

Local or community control has been proposed primarily by minority groups who have systematically been excluded from the consensus dominating American public policy in the past. The demand for community control is in essence a rejection of public services which are presumed to be under the control of majority interests in the larger society, and therefore prejudicial to the interests of a minority group which may predominate in a given locale.

For example, Friedmann advocates a "massive devolution of central governmental powers to decentralized territorial units." [19] This would make governmental programs more responsive to and more reflective of local needs and conditions. To enable local governments to carry out such responsibility, federally chartered nonprofit metropolitan development corporations are proposed to determine and carry out broad capital improvement programs in their respective regions. Recognizing that decentralization inevitably heightens group conflict, a new mission for planners or urban policy analysts would be to function as mediators "at the interfaces of group conflict to protect the system as a whole against increasing entropy."

[19] Friedmann, "The Future of Comprehensive Urban Planning," p. 323.

A second alternative for resolving the crisis in consensus is to use market mechanisms to deliver public services.[20] By giving clients the ability to purchase services in the market their bargaining position is potentially enhanced, presumably along with their ability to secure services which satisfy their needs. According to proponents of this approach, impersonal forces of the market make all major decisions in response to the will of the consumer, with business compelled by the profit motive to accept the market's decision. Recognizing that the market as it presently exists does not function this way, they argue for creation of a free market, based on competition and exchange. To accomplish this would require state regulation, a fact which brings us back to some form of centralized planning.

Criticisms of these proposed alternatives to centralized planning are discussed in Chapters 5 and 6. They rest on the assumption that public actions must be substituted for the pursuit of private interests in certain areas: (1) expressed individual needs that can be satisfied only by benefits which are indivisible (public goods), such as clean air and water, social equity and social stability, (2) indirect effects of individuals pursuing their own interests which adversely affect the interest of others (externalities), and (3) the needs of society which are not valued by individual consumers (merit wants), as in the case of preventive public health measures.

From one point of view the present crisis in finding and maintaining consensus results from too little centralized control rather than too much. This interpretation is supported by the active role of the judiciary in recent years in establishing operational policies. Federal and state court rulings have precipitated the development of new plans to assure civil rights, open housing, equal education, and environmental protection that attempt to rectify the failures of the established planning and policy-making process. Further evidence for the need for more authority is found in the strange anomaly that greater central-

[20] Milton Friedman, *Capitalism and Freedom* (Chicago, Ill.: University of Chicago Press, 1962).

ized control is being advocated in those systems which have traditionally been managed through the market, such as transportation, land development, and medical care, while market mechanisms are being advocated in those systems which have been highly centralized (at least at the local community level), most notably education and welfare.

We are brought back to the conflicting demands of the two essential aspects of central planning—control and consensus. Although "disjointed incrementalism" is ineffective and perhaps detrimental in terms of long-range goals, does it not assure a system of checks and balances, a diffusion of power? On the other hand, if central planning can more effectively meet broad social purposes through a rational delineation of priorities and allocation of resources, is the granting of the necessary power and authority to a central body a reasonable price to pay? The former position accepts limited problem solution and lack of a clear social purpose in order to maintain freedom in a pluralistic form of society. The latter appears to accept "authoritarian regimes of rational intervention in all aspects of social life, characterized by overall planning and total mobilization of energies to eradicate archaic social structures and install new ways of life and work." [21] For some this is tantamount to accepting a neofascism that may be more horrendous than the European form because of its basic foundation in technology.[22]

It is quite possible that many of these criticisms and countercriticisms are overstatements that need to be examined more carefully in the light of the experience of other countries. Both England and Yugoslavia were able to arrive at consensus and move on to a restructuring of the social order in a planned, systematic fashion. England's experience is relevant in that many of our social structures were shaped by the value system of that country. England, however, changed course twenty-five years

[21] Darcy Ribeiro, *The Civilization Process* (Washington, D.C.: Smithsonian Institution Press, 1968), p. 117.
[22] Bertram Gross, "Planning in an Era of Social Revolution," *Public Administration Review*, 31 (May–June, 1971), p. 287.

ago and we did not. The over-all concept of a British welfare state with its broad statement of social goals took shape as a result of World War II, though it should be recognized that the seeds for this change had been present for decades. The welfare state was an expression of a sense of direction, a statement of social reconstruction based on the realization that the war effort required a pooling of the country's resources and sharing of the risks by all.[23] It was, in fact, a blueprint of a social order, technical in its approach, identifying required resources and authority, that fits our definition of centrally planned change. We must keep in mind that this approach was initiated while the country was at war and that it was the "party platform" offered in a parliamentary election that gave the people a mechanism to express consensus or disagreement. Yet England today cannot be called an authoritarian state.

The experience in Yugoslavia was somewhat parallel, though the results somewhat different.[24] During the occupation of World War II, partisan activity depended on the cooperation of the whole country. The psychological effect of collective achievement and victory had a considerable impact on developments after the war. The main instrument of mobilizing and channeling resources necessary to fulfill the nation's goals was assumed to be the state. Because of the nature of the population, consisting largely of distinct ethnic or cultural groups, it would seem that consensus with regard to social purpose would be impossible to achieve. And yet, without outright dictatorship, some balance among diverse interests evolved. When early highly centralized planning efforts reflected problems, the locus of the planning was decentralized and mechanisms were established to assure integration with the national effort. The Yugoslavian experience is an example of Dror's megapolicy approach. Whether this is a function of the structure of planning developed in that country, or of the charismatic nature of politi-

[23] Beveridge Report, para. 459, *Social Insurance and Allied Services*, 1942.
[24] Eugene Pusic, "The Interdependence between Social and Economic Planning," *Social Welfare Policy*, ed. J. A. Ponsioen (S'Gravenhage: Mouton, 1962), p. 243.

cal leadership can only be tested after Tito. However, the last twenty-five years have demonstrated that centrally planned change can be acceptable to large numbers of people with different values and cultural backgrounds and can have positive results.

THE FUTURE FOR CENTRALLY PLANNED CHANGE

Given the dilemma posed by the twin requisites of control and consensus, is there need for centralized planning in the United States? Is it feasible? If so, what should its nature be and what institutional structures and technology does it require? In an effort to provide answers to these questions, this book has been organized around three objectives.

The first part of our study examines American experiences in centrally planned change. Planning for full employment, urban development, and health care will be analyzed in case studies. In examining these problem areas, we shall use the following questions as our guide:

1. To what extent has there been centralized planning in the United States on the federal level?
2. What conditions in America seem to facilitate centrally planned change, and what conditions mitigate against it (governmental structures, legal provisions, historical developments, social, economic, and political conditions)?

The second part of this book looks at theoretical alternatives proposed to eliminate some of the disadvantages of centralized planning. Foreign comparisons such as Yugoslavia's experimentation with decentralization are used. In evaluating these alternatives we pose the following questions:

1. What problems does decentralization solve? What problems does it leave unresolved?
2. To what extent can decentralization be incorporated into national approaches to planned change?

3. What problems does the private market solve? What problems does it leave unresolved?
4. To what extent can market mechanisms be used to serve public purposes and to meet social goals?

The book concludes with a consideration of the possibilities for centralized planning in the United States. What kind of functions should it perform? What kind of structure is necessary and possible within the American legal and cultural framework? What kind of technology is necessary for centrally planned change?

THE STRUCTURE FOR PLANNING

Questions about the structure for planning revolve in large part around the question, "Who shall do the planning?" All attempts to conceptualize the nature of centralized planning recognize the need for some public-regarding group responsible for conceiving and executing plans. This requirement reflects the more generalized problem of the distribution of power in society. For several decades it has been argued that liberal governments could not plan because of the inability to centralize decision-making. Critics have called for the creation of a group of planners above any special interest who could guide society without consideration for private gain.[25] Lowi argues for the creation of a senior civil service which would be beyond political influence and would be centralized to prevent allegiance to any given bureaucracy.[26] Such a cadre could assure that administrative decisions were clearly and objectively made and executed.

Assuming such proposals could be adopted, what should be the relationship between the formation of policy, the people or their sovereign policy-selecting apparatus, and this body of ex-

---

[25] Karl Mannheim, *Man and Society in an Age of Reconstruction* (New York: Harcourt, Brace, and World, 1940).

[26] Lowi, *The End of Liberalism*.

pert executors of policy? In effect, who shall establish the planner's goals?

If there is a need to control the power of such a group, does this require drastic rearrangements in our society, or can existing bodies such as the legislature be strengthened in their role as consensus-makers in establishing national policy? A number of writers [27] have developed this theme and see new functions and relationships for the existing branches of national government around the distinct tasks of policy formulation, execution, and evaluation.

This relationship between policy selectors and executors can be treated at a more mundane level. If general policies are approved by the Congress, with requisite authorization delegated to some executive office or planning unit, how much authority will actually be delegated? Historically, the Congress has not been content to write general purpose legislation, which authorizes funds without detailing constraints upon their use for a period of years. But lacking such a measure of delegation, each step in designing a plan or program and each adjustment made to fit practical needs must be sent back to the Congress for authorization. It is hard to see how central planning can become reality without some delegation of authority *and* resources to an execution unit with freedom to act as necessary to achieve the policy goals set forth in the sanctioning policy. Without some such continuity, planning becomes shooting at a constantly moving target as the successive interests of various groups rise and fall. The current flirtation with revenue-sharing, some feel, may create just such a situation at a subnational scale. Such efforts need to be carefully assessed to determine their impact on planning functions and structures.

Two models might be found in (1) the Department of Defense, whose plan capability, though annually scrutinized, has not been disrupted; and (2) the Social Security program, which has been shielded by the boundaries of actuarial mathematics.

[27] For example, see the writings of A. Etzioni and C. E. Lindblom.

14 *Centrally Planned Change*

Since many social planning problems lack the arcane protection of the actuary or the compelling interest of national security, can a comparable model be created for them? Is it possible to imagine a structure for social planning with the following characteristics:

1. Created by representatives of the citizenry to deal with some major sector of social concern (health, employment, and so on);
2. Shielded from annual shifts of political concern, yet accountable to policy-determining units of government such as the Congress;
3. With delegated authority, supported by allocation of funds sufficient for the purposes entrusted to it by the Congress and with freedom to distribute such funds to program agencies as necessary to achieve the policy results enunciated by the Congress.

The quandary over how to maximize both control and consensus (or accountability) reflected in discussions of the structure for planning suggests new functions or modes of operating. It is in this connection that the proposals for local control and market mechanisms have their greatest appeal. Planning strategies such as contextual planning do not prescribe the details of societal guidance but set the ground rules under which different interest groups operate.[28] Under this rubric, a mix of planning structures is proposed which incorporates public ownership as well as public supervision of private ownership. However the latter approach is only effective in those contexts in which competing interest groups are well balanced, as in the case of management and labor under the NLRB. It is relatively ineffective in contexts in which one party is relatively unorganized, as is the case with the Federal Communications Commission (FCC), the Interstate Commerce Commission (ICC), and the Civil

[28] This model is developed by A. Etzioni, *The Active Society*, as well as by John Friedmann, "The Future of Comprehensive Urban Planning," p. 323.

Aeronautics Board (CAB) in relation to consumers and private industry.

TECHNOLOGY OF PLANNING

The last major issue which needs exploration is the question of the appropriate tools of planning. The accepted notion of planning technology implies analytical tools such as systems analysis, benefit-cost analysis, cost-effectiveness, and forecasting. Such tools imply a considerable degree of centralized control. To what extent are they useful under less centralized conditions? Would other tools, such as licensing and pricing review used by regulatory agencies, and fiscal and monetary controls be more useful? Decision by adjudication, advocacy planning, and negotiation may better serve as planning techniques in more decentralized systems.

A third approach, one which has not been thought through, would encourage the achievement of public objectives through market choices of the individuals and groups being served. While Congress might wish to reserve for itself the function of earmarking purposes for which funds could be used, the consumers, not agencies, would hold the funds to command public services.

We seem to be faced with a serious dilemma in this country. Can we accept a desirable end—a rational, systematic approach to meeting human welfare needs—if the means to achieving this end require a change in the way our pluralistic system functions? Can we afford to continue operating with means which are widely acceptable but have little impact on preventing, controlling, or reversing the growth of social problems? Does centrally planned change always, by definition, result in use of undemocratic means of resource allocation and control? If planning continues to be incremental, and if the results of these efforts continue to offer questionable or intangible gains for large numbers of people, we may be faced with an internal upheaval that will move us toward centralized planning, as did the war for England and Yugoslavia. Is the destructive force of a crisis a prerequisite to finding consensus on our problems and accepting the idea of central planning? Or can we move toward a rational, systematic attack on social problems in an orderly fashion?

CHAPTER TWO

THREE AMERICAN EFFORTS AT CENTRALLY PLANNED CHANGE

This chapter contains three case studies of planning in relation to major social problems of national concern. We have attempted to provide some empirical basis for our subsequent discussion of theoretical issues in centrally planned change. For this purpose we have tried to select cases which represent typical efforts at national planning in the United States—in respect to the urban environment, employment, and mental health—in order to evaluate the saliency of the concept to the American scene. As such our cases reflect the complexity, the uncertain etiology, and the conflicting values inherent in the problems being addressed.

The case is a time-honored source of information and insight for the social sciences. What case studies lack in scientific precision is compensated for in the holistic view they provide of forces and values which shape social interaction in a particular situation. Case studies are often the seedbed for theories which can be further tested and which may serve to reshape ways of perceiving events about us.

The cases were prepared by specialists in their respective fields to provide a basis for the discussion of the more general questions asked in Chapter 1. Melvin M. Webber presents an evolutionary view of urban development. There follows the analysis by Robert A. Gordon of the development and effect of the government's full employment policy. The third case, drawn from the field of mental health, was developed from a variety of sources, including Thomas Plaut, Benjamin Pasamanick, Linda Norris, and Rae McNamara.[1] Unlike the rest of the book, these case studies reflect the writing style and social perspectives of their respective authors. In this way the reader can understand what data the original conference participants and authors worked with to build the reformulation of experience and theory stated in our concluding chapter.

These cases are not intended to be complete reconstructions of the planning efforts in each area. Rather each essay addresses itself to the skeletal outline of a planning problem and reveals the ambiguities and dilemmas which must be resolved if change is to be brought about by conscious design.

I. PLANNING THE URBAN ENVIRONMENT [2]

The course of city-building in America has been pursued without the aid of compass, map, rudder, or helmsman, and surely without a destination. Apparently it never occurred to anyone to do it otherwise. Until the new-town movement of recent days, cities were never conceived to be the designed-and-manufactured products of any corporation, public or private. Rather, they were but by-products of everyone's business—the residuals remaining from the conduct of the society's real business. Like other externalities of industrial processes, the clean-up job has been left to local governments to deal with as best they can—to tidy up the worst of the mess, possibly even to

[1] Linda Norris and Rae McNamara are Ph.D. candidates in community psychology at North Carolina State University.
[2] This case was prepared by Melvin M. Webber, University of California, Berkeley.

improve things a bit. But, because city-building is no one's af-fair, because cities develop as the consequences of billions of atomistic decisions, made by millions of deciders, over a long period of time, governments' efforts have typically been reme-dial and marginal. Their governance processes have been in-herently adaptive and evolutionary. Central planning styles of the sorts that might fit an authoritarian organization do not match the structure of the city development process. Neither the hierarchical command-chain nor the goal-consensus of an army or that of a small business firm can be found here.

Other modes of planning have developed, modes that seek to deal with whole systems while accepting the atomistic decisions and pluralistic traits of the polities that comprise the city. And the modes that seem to have worked best have not been the ones that city governments could direct.

It will be my thesis that, by happenchance, we hit upon an effective strategy for city-building. In future decades, when the currents in contemporary American history will have further eroded the capacities of local governments to deal with the problems and opportunities of urbanization, the task will fall to governments that are not territorially constrained. Rising socie-tal scale, increasing pluralism, and the emergence of a service economy are reinforcing the nationalization of urban society. In turn they are compelling styles of governance that are simulta-neously highly centralized (because they are located in national government) and highly decentralized (because they are depen-dent upon individuals' decisions). The new pluralism and the fast pace of change are already eliminating whatever "right an-swers" people may have once held to. A society comprising thousands of minority groups is going to have to invent a style of governance and planning that can protect each minority's own image of rightness by providing differentiated public facili-ties and services, by nurturing cultural diversity, and by en-couraging experimentation. As a start, it must find ways of ex-panding the range of options open to individuals and groups.

With so little known in the social and behavioral sciences that can feed into social policy, planning must become a process of social learning, appraising the outcomes of experiments and experience, and feeding its findings back into the decision channels. But even if we could do all that, there is still no gainsaying what sort of urbanization pattern should be sought after. The task of the planning system is to find that direction.

THE PLANLESS TRADITION OF CITY-BUILDING

The most remarkable trait of the city-building processes in America is their fantastic success in the absence of any sort of deliberate guidance system. There has been no national urbanization policy in America. Neither the Congress nor any other federal agency has ever enunciated guidelines for the locations of city settlements, for their compositions, their sizes, their growth rates, their layouts. And yet, thousands of settlements have been built, some of huge size and incredible complexity. Within some rather narrow limits of tolerance, they have grown to supply roughly the volumes of housing appropriate to the population sizes and characteristics; urban populations have been distributed among them roughly in scale with volumes of jobs; transportation and communication equipment have been installed, usually with channel capacities that are just barely adequate; shops have developed supplying millions of different commodities in just about the amounts for which residents express demands; and so on. Without any sort of plan or conscious intention, an elaborate and complex system of cities has been constructed, matching the demands of the national economy and the workings of the society, and with a closeness of fit that suggests some sorts of sensitive guidance systems must have been at work.

City-building processes seem to have been highly ordered. They appear to have been governed by self-sensing, self-organizing, self-regulating, and error-correcting processes that have been very effective. Where housing supplies have been deficient, new houses have gotten built. Where water systems have been inadequate, new supplies have gotten installed. Where new industries have emerged, new cities have developed in places that satisfy the new locational requirements; and they have come complete with people, buildings, communication lines, and the rest.

Of course the fits are never as good as some would like them to be. Many would contend there has never been an adequate supply of decent, safe, and sanitary housing; that sewerage systems have never been good enough; that large American cities have never incorporated the qualities of livability of which we are capable. I am quick to agree with those appraisals. It is true that the cup has been half empty. But I find it more telling, by far, that it has been half full.

If we could discover how the city-building processes have worked—how in the absence of a deliberate plan, such intricately complex systems have been built—we may then uncover the clues to a planning system that might work to fill the cup the rest of the way. Of one thing we can be sure: the planning styles we have tried in the past have been ineffectual, and we sorely need some more effective guidance systems. Later in this study a cybernetic planning style is introduced that might work in sympathy with the self-organizing and self-regulating processes of the economic markets and the political forums. Some suggestions for such a style are to be found in the record of intervention of our past urbanization history.

None of America's city-building success happened by magic. None of the intricate physical plants and complex social systems sprang forth without the willful application of purpose and intelligence. Cities get put together piece by piece, as individuals and groups construct the segments that suit their respective and particularistic purposes. In America's history, cities have not been built as designed wholes; nor have their locations or compositions been determined by informed, knowledgeable, and/or wise planners located at some central command post. As I noted at the outset, we have never had anything even pretending to be a national urbanization policy or program. And yet, many of the deliberate acts of national government have had pervasive and profound influence upon city-development processes.

Perhaps the most profound of the inducements to city-building were the congressional acts in mid-nineteenth century which triggered a revolution in agricultural productivity and opened the West to development. Land-grant and homestead legislation created an agricultural research and extension activity and a land-cultivation pattern that, jointly, resulted in an explosion in farm production that, in turn, fostered migration and a shift from farming to urban occupations. In parallel, encouragement of immigration from other continents led to rapidly growing urban populations at those cities where expanding factories found ready access to raw materials and transport. The congressional incentives to the extension of railroad lines fostered the spread of economic enterprise westward, and cities developed at raw material sites or at transport junctures where trans-shipment or break of bulk activities called for a labor supply.

None of these urban outcomes was in any sense planned, however. It was intended that agricultural productivity be expanded, but it was not intended (perhaps not even envisioned) that improved farming techniques would lead to city expansion. The aims of railroad construction were probably rather more direct; the railroad companies themselves sought to establish chains of new towns along their tracks in an effort to encourage freight shipments and to profit from sale of their large landholdings. But it would be something of an exaggeration to view any of these developments as the outcomes of any sort of national intention to build cities. Rather, the outcomes were seen as either fortuitous windfalls, when the consequences were profitable, or as unfortunate but necessary side-effects of progress.

And so it has been with a large assortment of congressional actions, directed to other ends, but profoundly affecting city-building. In recent times the Federal Housing Authority (FHA) mortgage-insurance program was implemented in the interest of fostering homeownership, a house-building industry, and mortgage-lending institutions. But it had the further, and more important, effect—probably unintended and maybe even unanticipated—of creating extensive, low-density suburbs around each of the major cities. In turn, suburbanization has led to large changes in life patterns and to what may be the most difficult of the urban problems of our time: the spatially extensive segregation of metropolitan populations by race and social class. The restructuring of life styles and of metropolitan spatial arrangements with the consequent restructuring of social relations was abetted by several other congressional actions that were taken without plan or without forecasts of latent outcomes. The highway construction program has certainly been a major contributor, for it made the suburbs accessible to each other and to the center-city job pools. The income tax provisions that favor homeowners, via permissible deductions of local property taxes and mortgage interest payments, reinforced the FHA incentives and consequences. The capital gains provisions gave advantage to those who built or bought and resold apartment properties, which in turn fostered suburban resettlement of single-person households. The fast depreciation provisions of federal procurement contracts encouraged those fortunate manufacturers to build spacious new plants in outlying suburban districts by lowering plant-building costs. In further turn, suburban municipalities have been subsidized in their efforts to install sewerage systems and to develop parks and other open spaces. And in many of these efforts, the federal programs have been reinforced and supplemented by similar ones installed by state governments.

An uninformed outsider, say one from a Scandinavian country, looking in upon the urbanization history of the past five decades, could easily draw the inference that deliberative central planning had been single-mindedly promoting suburbanization at the major metropolitan settlements. The most dramatic noncompatible program would seem to have been the urban-renewal efforts to rebuild the old centers and the earlier public-housing programs that were aimed at making the city habitable for the poor. The failure of urban renewal to stem the suburban movement might be construed as part of a national policy of suburban growth. And so too might the efforts to house black and poor folk in central cities, for the resulting concentration of lower-class minorities has been a forceful generator of suburbanization of upper-, middle-, and working-class whites. To an outsider, it might appear that the national urban growth plan envisaged has been a great success, so consistent have been the outcomes of various congressional programs.

Our visitor would surely also infer that our national rationality had determined upon a westward movement of the populations, upon the emptying of the continental central regions, the industrialization of the Old South, the intensive development of the Far West, and the construction of several major new metropolitan concentrations along the crescent extending from Florida through Arizona and up the West Coast. So many federal governmental programs have reinforced these changes, a rational observer would be forced to conclude that the changes were centrally planned and rationally intended. Only we natives know how foolish such an inference would be.

Among the dramatic forces affecting urban expansion along that crescent, federal military and space expenditures may have been the most powerful. It would be hard for our outside friend to avoid the conclusion that NASA, and perhaps Congress, was deliberately bent upon affecting some sorts of fundamental changes in the culture and politics of the South, so insistent were they upon locating key space installations and supplier plants there. But, whether intended or not (and some officials have emphatically denied such Machiavellian purpose), the effects have been the same. Nontraditional types of residents and industries have settled there, assumed political leadership roles, exercised voting rights, and contributed to the modernization of the local economy, society, and polity. In parallel, the favored treatment accorded research and development establishments and manufacturers in California has undoubtedly been as powerful a force in shaping population growth curves there as has any other single influence, sunshine included. During recent years some 32 percent of all military research and development contracts were awarded to California firms and 26 percent of the National Aeronautics and Space Administration (NASA) contracts. When contrasted with the fact that only 10 percent of the nation's population lives in California, the skew is clear. William Alonso concludes that the drift to the West was a direct consequence of military activity:

> The United States has been engaged in major wars in Asia for the greater part of three decades. That this has had a major effect on the development of the West Coast is so obvious it is often overlooked. The point need not be belabored, except to stress its magnitude: with the possible exception of the continuing agricultural revolution, it is probably the most significant factor that has affected the distribution of people and activities for the past one third of a century.[3]

Of course, no one would imply that Congress or anyone else had used warfare as an instrument of urbanization policy, but the outcome is nonetheless clear. The transportation and communications accessibilities that now link Asia with all parts of the nation did not require the localization of all war-making activities along the West Coast, of course. Indeed, many of the most closely linked activities did not find a locational advantage in California but remained in places like Long Island, Detroit, and Boston instead. California has been favored for other reasons in addition to proximity to the Pacific Ocean, many of them associated with the amenities of climate and landscape and with its nontraditional character that permitted experimentation and innovation. Our visitor would not be unreasonable to infer a congressional and bureaucratic intent to relocate

[3] William Alonso, "Problems, Purposes, and Implicit Policies for a National Strategy of Urbanization," Institute of Urban and Regional Development, University of California, Berkeley, Working Paper No. 158 (August, 1971), p 26. The careful reader of both Alonso's essay and this one will detect the degree of my debt to him.

a tenth of the nation's population in new California cities built with federal assistance. He would nonetheless be quite wrong. For the plain fact is that California just happened, that America has never had an urban-growth policy that was explicit.

If there has been implicit policy imbedded in the various legislative acts that have affected city growth, it has been non-conscious policy, hence scarcely warranting the policy label. If there was ever a consistent set of underlying objectives, it was probably a disposition favoring growth per se—a diffuse sense that more is better, taller is better, bigger is better. That is not an urban policy, of course, but, whenever there was sufficient analysis to suggest that some other policy contributed to city *growth*, that may have been enough to provoke positive congressional response.

Through it all, then, it appears that American urbanization has been planless, unintended, undirected. It has been the outcome of a great many governmental subpolicies concerned with agriculture, economic development, transportation, banking, education, and so on, but never of a plan dealing with the city-building outcomes of these more particularistic policies. And yet, despite the blindness of our city-building effort, the particularistic market processes that have underlain it have been adaptive to shifting preferences among consumers and shifting demands of the business and industrial sectors. American city-building has been reactive and adaptive. However far from perfect, however much better it might have been under some other guidance conditions, it has resulted in the construction of a complex system of cities that works remarkably well.

One is led to wonder how we might have improved upon the process and the outcomes had there been a central urban-planning agency with central government powers. Or had there been local governmental powers of greater effectiveness. Or had there been better intelligence available to private and public decision-makers. One cannot avoid asking whether there is a better system for building cities than the one that has yielded the great ones that planlessness built. I shall want to argue that, as if by accident, we hit upon some indirect modes of governance that were the effective ones. I believe we did it right, in not trying to plan whole cities as some other nations have done and as authoritarian rulers did in prior ages. And particularly in coming decades, when some fundamental changes are likely to be affecting American society, a mode of planning that seeks to shape the large-system context, rather than to make detailed developmental decisions, is likely to be the right one. But let me return to that argument in a moment. It is first necessary to identify some of the larger historical shifts that will affect the setting for future planning.

SOME LONG-TERM SOCIETAL DRIFTS

Three large societal changes seem to be underway that are likely to affect modes of governance and planning in future decades and to shape the process of urbanization as well. The *rising scale of the society* is fast converting America into an integrated, national urban system. The *changeover to the service economy* is already triggering an array of fundamental changes in the structure and behavior of the economy and in consumers' demands for social services. The *increasing pluralism* of high-scale, postindustrial society is loosing an array of political movements in defense of equity for the many new minorities, and the new pluralism is likely to generate an ever larger array of ethical issues for policy-makers.

Increasing Societal Scale

The natural outgrowth of increasing division of labor is increased interdependence among the specialized strangers who are working participants in the society. So finely divided are occupational and other social roles, and so interwoven is the matrix of the social economy, that it is only slight exaggeration to suggest that nearly everyone in the nation is, in at least some small degree, dependent upon everyone else.

At a time when the waves of repercussions from any action spread rapidly and far, huge errors are easily made before corrective actions can be taken. Large organizations with the capability of making large investments thus bear a large responsibility to anticipate the consequences of their actions upon the various publics those consequences will affect. Big oil tankers make big oil spills. Worldwide application of DDT rapidly affects animal life throughout the globe and with long-lasting effects. Large-development firms quickly set the pattern for urban development for a long time and over large areas. Increased size and increased connectivity require improved means of forestalling the worst of the external social costs that are now possible. No longer are the externalities of industrial activities mere "neighborhood effects," as they used to be called. Or, if so, the neighborhoods must now be reckoned as worldwide in extent.

The synoptic effect has been so intimately to integrate the economies, polities, societies, and geographies of the nation as to make the entire country the equivalent of a single city. Yet we continue to believe and act as though settlements of the late twentieth century are like those of prior eras when each settlement's society was separate from that of others.

The Service Economy

The proportion of jobs in the service industries has risen to about 60 percent, and the fastest growing sector under this heading embraces knowledge-building functions—education, research and development, and others growing out of the boom in science and technology. The contemporary cities of America were built primarily to meet the demands of industrial society, with all its reliance upon bulky products and heavy freight movements. We have some signals from places like Phoenix, Houston, Los Angeles, and San Jose that the postindustrial city that might match the service economy will have far different requirements, but we have yet to discover its critical details.

This ambiguity and uncertainty about the right way to build future cities must fundamentally condition the style of planning we adopt. We need a planning style that is intrinsically experimental and has the capability of learning from experience. If we are to find what sorts of cities match the workings of a service society, we are going to have to solicit responses from that society. Any other way is likely to be incompatible with that society. The traditional way of designing a future city, by "remembering the answers," [4] is bound to failure.

Expanding Pluralism

America has always been a highly pluralistic nation. Despite rapid acculturation to urban styles of behavior and thought, and despite the Americanization of the immigrants and their children, the original national differences have remained. So, too, have religious affiliations and regional identifications. As Glazer and Moynihan have described the ethnic groups of New York, it appears that the melting pot did not work as many had expected. [5]

Yet, despite the differences among the many immigrant groups at the end of the last century, they may have been more homogeneous in their culture traits than are their great grandchildren today. Peasant peoples shared many thoughtways and behavioral patterns, even though geographically isolated from each other. [6] Moreover, they had little chance to be different from their parents. With life opportunities tightly constrained

---

[4] The phrase is the title of Nathan's Glazer's anthology on the student revolt, published by Basic Books in 1970.

[5] Nathan Glazer and Daniel Patrick Moynihan, *Beyond the Melting Pot* (Cambridge, Mass.: MIT Press and Harvard University Press, 1963).

[6] The extensive literature around this theme is summarized in Marc Fried, "Transitional Functions of the Working Class Communities," in *Mobility and Mental Health*, ed. M. Kantor (New York: D. Van Nostrand, 1974). It is also reviewed in Melvin M. Webber and Carolyn C. Webber, "Culture, Territoriality, and the Elastic Mile," in *Taming Megalopolis*, ed. C. W. Eldredge (Garden City, N.Y.: Anchor Books, 1967), vol. 1, pp. 35–53.

and with future conditions uncertain at best, they lived perforce in the styles that were current, and that had been current for centuries.

In the modern high-scale and knowledge-rich society, quite the opposite conditions pertain. Each successive generation conflicts and competes with its predecessor, and the rewards go to those who are different. The contemporary youth are actively experimenting with new modes of thought, with new religions, new family structures, new music, new art, new styles of governance, new moralities, and more. The extent of variation and exploration is limited only by their imaginations. The traditional constraints of the folkways and mores of their ancestors are rapidly weakening.

But it is not only the youth who celebrate difference, of course. Large segments of adult populations are experimenting with a variety of educational programs, art forms, recreational activities, literatures, and other media that have made them different from *their* parents. If they are also conformists, sharing beliefs and behaviors with others in their own adult social groups, they are nonetheless nonconformists within some larger population set. It looks as though the herald of a coming mass society, so loudly proclaimed in the fifties, was wrong. In place of the mass society, we seem instead to be evolving an increasingly pluralistic one, in which each individual belongs to social groups which have norms that are peculiarly their own. The most explicit expressions of the sameness of a mass society—the communications media, the ubiquitous advertising industry, the franchised motels, restaurants, and food distributors—are but surface manifestations. The same transportation revolution that has muted differences growing out of geographic separation has allowed locational freedom to large numbers of citizens for the first time in history. Footlooseness has led to unexpected patterns of city settlement and growth of spatially dispersed, nonplace communities of interest and their rise to new positions of power. This development is likely to foster the emergence of rather different styles of planning and governing.

Nonplace Communities and Nonterritorial Governments

In the milieu of a national urban society composed of variously differentiated groups, traditional bases for community structure are weakening. The social organization that at one time coincided with the boundaries of village or town is yielding to the spatially extensive social organization which defines its members to accord with their interests, rather than their locations.[7]

All manner of interest-based groups are forming that are national in scale, as indicated by geographic distribution of their members and by the kinds of substantive topics that occupy them. The obvious examples include the trade associations, labor unions, churches, civic societies, corporations, even local businessmen's clubs, such as the Rotarians who boast of their internationalism. A striking feature of these kinds of organizations is that they have taken on the characteristics of governments. These interest-based communities are able to tax their members, to constrain individuals' behavior when they violate the group's norms, to impose sanctions for nonconformity; and they of course act positively on behalf of their members' special interests. They may have legislative bodies to set policy and activate programs, executive branches to carry on the day-to-day business of the organization and to represent the collective interest, and judiciaries to adjudicate differences and to assess proprieties. The American Medical Association, the Motor Vehicle Manufacturers Association, and the United Auto Workers are each a government for the selected groups that comprise its members and within the specialized substantive domains over which they grant it jurisdiction.

These differ from public governments in a fundamental way, however. Most public governments are territorially defined,

---

[7] I have explored this phenomenon in several essays, most directly in "The Urban Place and the Nonplace Urban Realm," in M. M. Webber, *et al.*, *Explorations into Urban Structure* (Philadelphia, Pa.: University of Pennsylvania Press, 1964) and in "The Post-City Age," *Daedalus*, 97 (Fall, 1968), pp. 1091–1110.

whereas most private ones are not. With origins in the distant past, when land as soil was the main source of sustenance, when membership in a society was determined solely by place of birth-and-residence, and when invasion of the society's territory by outsiders was a threat to sheer survival, jurisdictions of public governments were inherently and necessarily delineated in the language of territory. Each kingdom, and, later, each republic claimed jurisdiction over the men and affairs that fell within the land area the government ruled over. The primal function of those governments in agrarian times and in times of intertribal and international warfare was protective, and the best protection was a secure frontier and a well-defended landscape.

Whenever the social community coincided in space with the geographic terrain, jurisdiction over both land area and communal affairs could appropriately be assigned to the same government. Those conditions prevailed over most of the world during most of human history. With the availability of means of transport and increased mobility in recent centuries, the territorial principle for delineating governmental jurisdictions has been progressively eroded, and may already be dysfunctional.

The American constitutional basis of territorial definition of states, counties, and municipalities is, at best, becoming anachronistic. No state threatens to invade the turf of another; no city need worry about protecting cultivated soil; few social communities are any longer spatially coincident with the territorial lines defining a public government's jurisdiction. But most difficult of all, few of the problems that are manifested at any given place have their origins at that place. Thus, place-defined and place-constrained governments find themselves impotent to deal with the conditions within their spaces. The incredible thing about it is that few officials seem to recognize that simple fact, but continually turn to such inappropriate devices as model-city, neighborhood-based programs, community action programs, and the like. One of the striking fantasies of our time has been the resurgence of localism in an attack on some of the underlying structural difficulties of the national society. Another is the facility with which the public holds mayors responsible for social ills.

The garbage collection problem in New York City is not a problem spawned by New Yorkers and susceptible to solution by mayors or city departments. It is a reflection of the affluences of the time, the technologies of solid waste management, and the culture of central city populations. None of these conditions is peculiar to any specific city; none has its origins in cities at all, individually or collectively. The fiscal plight of the Newarks and New Yorks is similarly a consequence of the workings of events that are not specific to any city or space. High welfare costs reflect the conditions in the regional and national economies, the deficient educational opportunities afforded children years before in other states, the various discriminatory practices for whose complex social histories no city government can rationally be held liable, and so on. Clearly, it is rather silly to suppose that any city agency might "solve" the problems of unemployment or underemployment; or that it might, through local interventions, "resolve" the problems of poverty; or that it might significantly affect income distribution; or that it might get at the causes of drug addiction; or indeed, that it might do anything curative about crime or any of a long list of social and economic difficulties that are made manifest in city settings. Typically, these most intractable difficulties are large-system problems with roots buried deep within the matrixes of the whole society. The fact is we know almost nothing about the etiologies of these social conditions. Many of them may yield to no known therapies. Some might be alleviated through activities of international agencies, if, as with some physical diseases, we know something of their epidemiologies. At this time in history, the national government, as the least territorially constrained and largest of the public governments in the nation, is the structure offering the most effective means of approach to this scale of problems.

I am guessing that the rising societal scale, the emergence of a nationally integrated economy-polity-and-society, and the increasingly complex network of interlocking and spatially extensive interest-based communities have all been contributing to the new roles the federal government has been accumulating during the past forty years. I am guessing, too, that the shift to the information- and knowledge-fueled service economy is now going to be further eroding the roles of local governments, placing still further demands upon the national government.

In an open and mobile society of large scale, persons move about easily from place to place. Investments made in their education and training are carried with them, and local governments which paid for the educational costs are thus deprived of the potential returns. The state of Mississippi, which invests generously in 'Ole Miss' on behalf of her native sons, is short changed when the best graduates migrate to the greater opportunities of New York or Los Angeles. But on the other side of the coin, her failure to invest adequately in the education of Negro children redounds to the disbenefit of New York and Los Angeles, for Negroes also migrate but frequently enter the welfare rolls.

One approach to the problem posed by local governmental profits and losses caused by investment in mobile human resources is to charge the bills against the whole society's account. That may be why Congress has recently accepted responsibility for funding preschool, elementary, secondary, and higher education, traditionally local functions. That is also why the federal government must become the banker for the welfare system, as it has for social security, and why it must be the custodian of a national health insurance program as well. Since one can never be sure where the incidences of benefits and costs of any specific human investment will fall within the geographic space of the nation, our response has been to place the national government in the banker role. By thus moving to the next larger whole system, externalities are internalized; and we can eliminate the impossible accounting problems of transferring compensatory payments to losing publics from those who profit.

It would seem that there is a somewhat stronger case for local financing of such place-fixed investments as roads, sewers, and parks. None of these is readily moved once installed. But the federal government has also taken on responsibilities for these as well as the human services. If there is a clear rationale, it might be partly justified by the same mobility among population groups. Newcomers who have use of an installed urban freeway system, for example, would otherwise not have contributed to its installation costs had the costs been borne solely by local residents. Of course, if that line of reasoning were extended, there would be very little left to be financed by local governments. I am guessing that this could happen.

The signals announcing that the federal government has already assumed new responsibilities are unmistakable. In the 1954 Brown decision the Supreme Court asserted that educational policy, long the most cherished province of local government, was no longer solely a local matter. Later Congress, in passing the Elementary and Secondary Education Act, and four presidents who had responsibilities for administering court orders and congressional programs, firmly established the federal role. The decision of the California Supreme Court in *Serrano* v. *Priest*, and parallel cases in other states, is having a similar effect, this time passing education-policy and education-funding responsibilities to state governments.[8] Recent decisions in Richmond, Virginia, and Detroit calling for integration in the schools on a metropolitan-wide scale are a still further challenge to the autonomy of local governments.[9]

---

[8] *Serrano* v. *Priest.* 5 Cal. 3d 584, 487 P. 2d 1241 (1971). This decision of the California Supreme Court requires the State Board of Education to adopt a school financing plan that equalizes tax expenditures among school districts. A similar ruling by the United States District Court for West Texas was overturned by the United States Supreme Court. *Rodriguez* v. *San Antonio Independent School District*, 337 F. Supp. 280 (1971).

[9] *Bradley* v. *School Board of Richmond, Virginia*, 462 F. 2d 1058 (1972), 93 S. Ct. 1952 (1973); *Bradley* v. *Mulliken*, 42 U.S.L.W. 2022 (C.A. June 12, 1973).

This transfer of governing authority to the largest governmental organization is quite the right response to the rising scale of the larger society. In a society whose integral members are geographically dispersed but whose central concerns are not of a geographic sort, only the least territorially bounded of our public governments can provide the governing and planning guidance.

Over forty years now the federal government has been moving, almost systematically, into an expanding array of policy and programmatic fields. This movement represents an appropriate adaptive response to the rising scale of the society and to the declining localism of the plural polity. Simultaneously, the many private governments have been occupying the same or parallel topical fields, again as an adaptive response to the nationalization of their separate publics and to the integration of the national society. If a physician cares about the conditions of medical insurance or about the most recent research findings in his specialized field, he cannot of course limit his attention to his county medical society. Medicine is a national affair, at least. To limit one's attention to any smaller realm is to make oneself ineffectual.

PROSPECTS FOR A MATCHING PLANNING STYLE

Expanding roles for the national governments, public and private, and declining ones for local governments are not necessarily equivalent to increasing centralization of authority and decision-making. One can imagine a governing and planning style in which the rise of the national governments and the demise of municipalities would lead to increasing dependence upon atomistic and individualistic decision processes and to rising degrees of personal freedom. The outlook for such a happy development is not very bright, of course. If forced to make a high-odds prediction, I would be compelled to an Orwellian image. But, with the hope of forestalling that dismal prospect, let us explore an alternative to it.

In Search of Expanded Choice

One seemingly simple organizing principle for such a planning-and-governing system would require that central-agency decisions be designed to open the range of options accessible to individuals and groups. As I have intended to suggest above, the increasing pluralism of the nation's publics is making for ever expanding diversity in cognitive, behavioral, and living styles and for an ever widening array of preferences. If publicly provided services and if regulatory practices are to accord with those trends, they must be inherently choice-opening.

That trait would make them quite different from the ones that have become traditional in the public services, and rather in contrast with the styles of the welfare states of Northern Europe which many Americans are seeking to emulate. Instead of providing services and facilities in standardized formats judged by professionals in government to be decent, or good, or right, the aim would be to permit consumers to select from an array of types those they happen to prefer. Programs directed to supplying improved housing for poor families would be more likely to satisfy their varied preferences if the families were provided with the money directly, rather than with government-designed and -built houses at subsidized rent levels in the Swedish manner. Rather than efforts to improve the quality of television service in the BBC manner, a program aimed at easing entry into the industry would help assure diversity of program content and permit viewers to elect program styles. In this instance a solution may be at hand, for cable television could supply the medium for converting an oligopolistic industry into a competitive one, while relieving governmental agencies of any responsibility for program content.

Government agencies have historically done a poor job as direct producers of goods and services. Like nongovernmental monopolies, they tend to produce a standardized product. Standardization in the public schools is a notable example.

Even governmental regulation of private producers too easily turns into setting minimum product-standards which become maximum, witness the FHA house. Instead of the typical reflex reaction of government—creating a new agency—I propose that government offer incentives to generate new firms.

Standards That Unstandardize

Standards are certainly required, but they are standards of a different sort from the product- or service-specification we have been employing so rampantly. Standards of weights and measures, standards for screw threads, standards for numbers of lines in television pictures, spacing of electrodes in a household outlet, railroad gauge, and the many others of these sorts are of a different caste from the curricular standards of schoolboards or the building codes of municipal governments. When all manufacturers make screws to the same profiles and thread counts, a great many permutations of different manufacturers' parts become possible. Machines and components can then be recombined in nearly infinite ways, and users thus have far greater ranges of options open to them than if each manufacturer had his own peculiar screw design.

Similarly, by agreeing to use the twenty-six–letter Roman alphabet and the ten-base Arabic numeric system, virtually everyone profits from the array of options that are opened. Again recombination of incredible variety is possible, permitting a highly varied literature and allowing individuals to put together their own messages, to compile their own accounts, and to share their knowledge with unlimited audiences. The alphabet follows the principle first discovered by Mother Nature when she found that unlimited genetic variations could be wrung from but four letters in the genetic alphabet. Here is standardization with a difference: standardization whose intrinsic capacity is to promote difference!

Governments have been most effective when they have followed this style of leadership and regulation. Whether by promoting interchange, as with the adoption of weights and measures and common languages (including the new machine languages, of course), by promoting interchangeability of parts, as with machine standards of the sort I have been noting, or by promoting competition, as through the enforcement of the anti-trust legislation, the effects have been to foster differentiation and diversity. The policing of industry, by agencies such as the Food and Drug Administration and the Federal Trade Commission, has been most beneficial to society when fostering product differentiation and improvement rather than merely exposing fraud.

The test for the effectiveness of a governing process in these matters could be a rather simple one. If consumers had real options to choose on their own, many of the traditional types of quality tests could be abandoned. The assessor's question then should ask not whether the product or the service is good or right. Rather, it should ask, first, whether it is supplied in sufficiently differentiated assortment as to satisfy the preferences of diverse consumers, and, second, whether the secondary effects are such as to expand consumers' freedom to be different.

These two tests supply the clues to a style of planning and governing that could serve the plural publics in high-scale society. But there's a serious rub. To apply Nature's principle of language standards and the normative principle favoring differentiation is to require an inventive capacity that, so far, has been most commonly found in the nondeliberative, nonconscious patterns of discovery. Because neither planners nor anyone else in government headquarters is likely to be smart enough or inventive enough to think up all the game plans that would be required, let me suggest a mode of search that might work. To illustrate, we can return to our initial concern with national urbanization.

Strategy for National Urbanization Planning

I am not suggesting that a return to laissez-faire conditions is desirable nor do I believe that planless development is inherently superior. My observation is a more modest one: it notes that betterment comes from experimentation, and that the effective way to get experimentation in the city-building business is by encouraging the many individual participants in the city-building process to try out their ideas. Reliance on old ways is not likely to be good enough in a society that is changing as rapidly as this one. A permissive posture toward innovative and exploratory behavior is likely to lead to discovery or invention of new ways that could not be deliberately uncovered.

Individual businessmen have made locational and investment decisions within the context of these various governmental policies and programs. Home builders have constructed large sections of cities, in implicit partnership with governmental agencies, each of which builds its own specific facility type, and with the many private firms that have installed wholesale and retail outlets, business and personal service establishments, and so on. Piece by piece, individuals, firms, and governmental agencies have made atomistic decisions to accord with their respective purposes. Without a plan, typically with no over-all guidance, complex city structures have emerged. As I observed above, the degree of fit among the various subsystems has been truly remarkable. The modern American city may be as complex a physical-societal apparatus as exists outside nature. Its autonomous self-organizing character suggests that a planning system would do well to mimic its developmental processes.

After many years of search, we still do not have adequate theory that might expose causal relations between urban spatial structure and economic productivity, qualities of social life, potentialities for personal freedom, or any of an array of valuative criteria that might guide urbanization policy. If, some years ago, we had undertaken to formulate such a policy, nevertheless, and then deliberately had pursued programs aimed at shaping urban-growth patterns, I suspect we would have done far worse than we have.

Most other nations have followed the planned-urbanization course, at least nominally; and some, notably those in Northern

Europe, have effectively implemented it. As a consequence, they have indeed evolved different urban patterns than occurred in America.

Britain and Sweden have both undertaken to limit the size of their primate city and to redirect growth to new towns. Each has largely rebuilt its old housing stock through direct public action, typically replacing old tenements with apartment houses, many of them of the high-rise type. With slower growth of automobile use, each has rebuilt its rail-transit lines and suburban railroads, fostering transit patronage. Urban-renewal programs have been carried out far more extensively than in America. By now there are nearly thirty new towns in process in the United Kingdom, surely the most emphatic program of its kind in the Western world. In both nations the impact of national urban policy is visually apparent, as it is in Denmark and The Netherlands. The city stops at the green-belt, sometimes as a line of apartment houses abutting the meadows. Densities are typically high. Buildings and roads in new settlements are carefully placed; indeed new developments are site-planned in as minute detail as are the buildings themselves—typically all in the same central planning office. Here is city design at perhaps its most extreme form.

When British and Scandinavian city planners visit America they are characteristically appalled by what they interpret as rampant disorder. Our own intelligentsia has picked up the cry, and we now have a movement underway favoring new-town development.

And yet, it is by no means clear that the voluble criticisms of American urbanization are warranted or that even a massive new-town construction program will improve upon life opportunities in America. Surely, there is no evidence that British new-town residents are any better off than their countrymen living in other city types. As I have argued elsewhere, it is true that the new American cities do not fit any of our traditional paradigms of orderliness; but they are nonetheless highly structured and finely tuned to the workings of the economic, political, and social processes that comprise modern urban society.[10] More than that, they have evolved to match the operational characteristics of the new automobile-transportation system and the contemporary communications systems which have, in turn, been powerful forces shaping the cities. The postwar suburbs and postwar metropolitan areas have offered their residents opportunities to experiment with new styles of living that would be impossible in older style settlements—including styles of recreation, family relations, and neighborhood association. Los Angeles, Houston, Phoenix, San Diego, and the rest are late-industrial/early-postindustrial cities which probably conform to their residents' environmental and living preferences far more closely than did the older cities they migrated from. These are cities appropriate to the late twentieth century.

The cities of America emerged out of permissive tolerance for individualism, and especially in recent years, for the accoutrements of individualism: private automobiles, single family houses, personalized open space, and the opportunities for free association among members with like interests. America's newest cities are open and experimental. Except for the constraints imposed by a network of federal, state, and municipal regulations (zoning, building, traffic, and similar codes are examples), individuals are effectively encouraged to experiment with different styles of city subsystems, then to offer them to a relatively open market of option-free consumers. Some house styles are accepted; some fail the market test; and the builders go on to expand the supply of types that are most preferred. The suburbs and cities have thus evolved in patterns that would have come off no planner's drawing board. No one could have deliberately invented the Sunset Strip (or Piccadilly Circus for that matter—prior to the redevelopment plan, that is). No political leader would have approved so unusual a proposal as scattered high-rise office buildings, if an inventive planning of-

[10] The discussion appears as "Order in Diversity: Community without Propinquity" in *Cities and Space*, ed. Lowdon Wingo (Baltimore, Md.: Johns Hopkins Press, 1963).

fice had suggested it. No rational planner would have recommended that long-distance commuting by automobile be permitted—much less encouraged. I am guessing that under centrally controlled conditions, Los Angeles and Houston would not have happened in their present forms. And, if they had not, it is quite plausible to infer that they would not have been nearly as prosperous and successful as they have.

The main difficulties of the laissez-faire policy in urban development reside in the several conditions under which no markets can exist and where large-system consequences are undesired. The first set includes the situations where externalities must be somehow forestalled or compensated, where merit goods are sought, where investment requirements are so large or where risks are so great that private capital is not attracted, and where public goods must be supplied. All these circumstances command the intervention of public governments, sometimes as sole suppliers. (The classical lighthouse will get built only if some solitary public enterpriser makes it happen.)

The second difficulty with laissez-faire strategies derives from the likely prospect that the sum of individually satisfactory atomistic choices may be a wholly undesirable collective outcome. Or, the mirror of that: a desired collective outcome may be attainable only through collective action. Especially in a high-scale society, where events in one place may intimately affect persons in distant places and where repercussions of individual actions can be huge and rapidly diffused, large-system effects occasionally may be of overriding importance. In the face of a large and impending smallpox epidemic, for example, no one would turn to privatized methods of prevention.

The difficulty comes with knowing when collective ends should govern and when they unduly constrict private ones, when consensus by majorities becomes tyranny over minorities, when mutual agreement unnecessarily constrains innovation and experimentation. With cultural pluralism making for ever widening values pluralism, who is to say what is right?

The conclusion cannot be for hands-off, but neither can it be for control by the heavy-handed. The best way, I contend, is to deny there is a best way.

Centralized planning might be an effective means of defending that principle, and, simultaneously, of assuring that the test for choice-expansion gets consistently applied. Its underlying style would be permissive, encouraging the invention of new alphabets that would in turn generate new variety. It would be simultaneously alert to new developments and to impending difficulties, maintaining a sensitive intelligence antenna and network system, directed to monitoring outcomes of public and private programs and to feeding back forecasts and findings to those who care. Essentially a cybernetic guidance system devoted to accelerating social learning, such a planning process need not design the details of services and facilities, only the contexts for them. Long on permissiveness and short on constraint, it would only regulate the settings within which individuals and groups produce and consume those services and facilities with the objective of regulation being to assure that irregularity and diversity result.

In those senses, the planning system might indeed be "centralized." But the centralization-decentralization dichotomy does not really fit. Perhaps it might be better characterized as systemic, being simultaneously oriented to whole systems and their parts, to collective ends and to private ones, and to the evolutionary, systemic processes by which cities emerge over time. But it cannot be authoritarian, for the only authority it can admit is a values pluralism of diverse publics and of the autonomous processes of development.

II. PLANNING FOR FULL EMPLOYMENT [11]

EVOLUTION OF THE FULL EMPLOYMENT GOAL IN THE UNITED STATES

No country explicitly avowed full employment as a policy goal before the Great Depression. During the 1930s, however, massive unemployment and the intellectual stimulus provided by the Keynesian Revolution spurred an increasing number of economists and research groups—particularly in England, Sweden, and the United States—to turn their attention to ways of achieving and maintaining full employment. The war also brought concern about the problems of postwar readjustment and a widespread resolve on both sides of the Atlantic that in the years ahead a paramount goal of public policy should be the maintenance of a high level of employment—of full employment.

One of the first of these national commitments to the goal of high employment was made by the British government in its *White Paper on Employment Policy,* issued in 1944. Sir William Beveridge referred to this White Paper as "a milestone in economic and political history." [12] In the United States, a comparable step was taken with the passage of the Employment Act of 1946. The phrase "full employment" is nowhere mentioned in the legislation, which, however, did pledge that the federal government would use "all practical means" to create and maintain "conditions under which there will be afforded useful employment opportunities . . . for those able, willing, and seeking to work, and to promote maximum employment, production, and purchasing power."

What rate of unemployment corresponds to full employment

[11] This case was prepared by Robert A. Gordon, University of California, Berkeley.

[12] William H. Beveridge, *Full Employment in a Free Society* (New York: Norton, 1945), p. 260.

in the United States? The early reports of the Council of Economic Advisors (which was created by the Employment Act) suggested a moderate range around 4 percent, but precise quantification of the employment target was avoided in all economic reports of the President prior to 1962. On the whole, it is probably fair to say that, between 1946 and 1961, official policy at least tacitly accepted a target in the neighborhood of 4 percent, but the target was not made explicit. One might say that a range rather than single figure served as a target—the range being from an unemployment rate slightly below 4 percent to an upper limit that at times was close to 5 percent.

The employment goal became much more explicit with the advent of the Kennedy administration. The 1962 *Economic Report of the President* used the specific figure of 4 percent. But this was to be only an interim goal with efforts directed at reducing the impact of structural unemployment to move the unemployment target steadily from 4 percent to successively lower rates. This policy continued into the Johnson administration.

At first, this also seemed to be the position of the Nixon administration, which began in 1968 when the national unemployment rate was below 4 percent. Indeed, there was a fleeting moment when it appeared as if this administration had set its sights higher than had its predecessor. In the 1970 *Economic Report of the President*, the Council of Economic Advisors projected the growth of potential output to 1975 on the assumption of an unemployment rate of 3.8 rather than 4 percent.

Official attitudes changed rapidly. Unemployment rose during the 1970 recession to a peak of 6.1 percent in December and remained stubbornly at about the 6 percent level during all of 1971, although the low point of the recession was reached in November, 1970. Increasingly, this effect was being explained by underlying structural changes which made it more difficult to achieve an unemployment rate of 4 percent without an unacceptable rate of inflation.

This new position was formally acknowledged in June, 1971, when the Secretary of Treasury characterized the 4 percent target for full employment as a "myth." And an increasing number of administration spokesmen began to suggest that for the time being we must accept a full-employment target corresponding to an unemployment rate of 4.5 percent or possibly higher.

This new attitude toward the full-employment target was strengthened by scholarly research that indicated a changing age-sex composition of the labor force. A particularly influential study in this connection was presented by George Perry at the Brookings Institution late in 1970,[13] and the changing age-sex composition of the labor force was again emphasized by the Council of Economic Advisors in the January, 1972, *Economic Report of the President.* Women and teenagers, with relatively high unemployment rates, had become a significantly larger fraction of the labor force over the last fifteen years; and prime-age males, who typically experience relatively low unemployment rates, had become a much smaller proportion of the labor force.

Against this background, the President introduced his new economic policy in August, 1971. Since 1969 inflation had not responded inversely to rising unemployment. Now it was important to reduce unemployment—although not necessarily to 4 percent—while at the same time retarding the still unacceptably high rate of increase in prices. The situation was made even more urgent by the drastic deterioration of the American balance of payments. The result was the wage-price freeze of Phase I and the wage and price controls of Phase II (as well as the decision to allow the dollar to float in foreign exchange markets until it found its new, lower value). The United States government had embarked on an unprecedented peacetime experience with a stringent incomes policy.[14]

[13] George L. Perry, "Changing Labor Markets and Inflation," in *Brookings Papers on Economic Activity,* Arthur M. Okun and George L. Perry, eds. 1970:3, pp. 411–441. See also the paper by Robert J. Gordon in *ibid.,* 1971:1, pp. 105–158.

[14] The Kennedy and Johnson administrations had used "jawboning" to induce business and labor to adhere to a set of guideposts, and to that extent a weak version of an

48 *Centrally Planned Change*

THEORETICAL BASES FOR AGGREGATIVE FULL EMPLOYMENT

As the above history points up, the goal of full employment in its purely aggregative aspects cannot be considered in isolation. Other goals—price stability, balance-of-payments equilibrium, and rapid economic growth—that loom large in the mind of the policy-maker may conflict with that of full employment.

It does no great violence to reality to combine some of these goals. Whatever contributes to price stability and reduces the rate of inflation is likely to contribute to balance-of-payments equilibrium. Similarly, maintenance of full employment means that the economy is growing at the rate made possible by its potential output. Thus, from the point of view of macro-economic policy, we can concentrate on the two goals of full employment and price stability. These goals *are* in conflict. The more closely we adhere to one, the further we move from the other.

The economist expresses this dilemma in terms of a welfare function. If we write

$$Z = f(U, \dot{P})$$

we are simply saying that economic welfare (Z) is a function of the national unemployment rate (U) and the rate of change in the price level ($\dot{P}$). Welfare increases as unemployment and inflation decrease.

But until recently, in the real world the rate of inflation tends to increase as unemployment declines. This relationship is summarized in the now famous "Phillips curve," about which a great deal has been written since A. W. Phillips published his original article in 1958.[15] The nature of the problem facing the policy-maker is illustrated in Figure 1. The curves XX' and X_1X_1' are two Phillips curves, applicable to a particular economy at two given times. XX' represents a less favorable situa-

incomes policy had been used before. Of course, direct wage and price controls had been used before in wartime.

[15] A. W. Phillips, "The Relation between Unemployment and the Rate of Change of Money Wages," *Economica*, 25 (November, 1958), pp. 283–300.

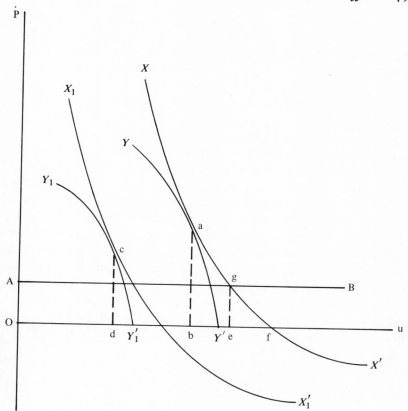

FIGURE 1. The Phillips curve of the relationship between price level (P) and unemployment (u).

tion than does X_1X_1'. Any given rate of inflation on the vertical axis such as OA involves a higher level of unemployment if the Phillips curve is XX' than if it is X_1X_1'.[16] A variety of factors

[16] In Figure 1, the vertical axis measures the rate of increase in prices. Strictly speaking, the Phillips curve shows the relation between unemployment and the rate of increase in *wages*, not prices. But there is, particularly in the longer run, a simple relation between the rates of increase in wages and in prices. The rate of increase in the price level is approximately equal to the rate of increase in average hourly compensation minus the rate of increase in man-hour productivity.

can cause the Phillips curve to shift; for instance, a change in the age-sex composition of the labor force may cause a shift of the Phillips curve to the right, thus making it more difficult to return to an unemployment rate of 4 percent without experiencing an unacceptable rate of inflation.

This brings us to the other pair of curves in Figure 1, YY' and Y_1Y_1'. These are indifference curves that represent the combinations of price stability and unemployment, all of which are acceptable to the decision-maker, that is, he is "indifferent" about the selection of any particular combination represented by the curve. A given indifference curve, say YY', reflects the policy-maker's conception of the balance between inflation and unemployment that will keep social welfare at the same level. The curve is concave to the origin. As unemployment increases and the rate of inflation declines, the policy-maker is less and less willing to accept more unemployment in order to continue the downward trend in prices.

Welfare increases as we move toward the origin in Figure 1. Thus Y_1Y_1' represents a higher level of welfare than YY'; every point on the former reflects a better combination of unemployment and inflation.

Given the Phillips curve—say, XX'—then welfare is maximized at the point where an indifference curve derived from the welfare function is tangent to the Phillips curve. This would be at point a. Without some change that shifts the Phillips curve, welfare cannot be increased by accepting either more inflation or more unemployment than that represented by point a.

Structural and Frictional Aspects of the Full Employment Goal

We turn now to the structural aspects of employment policy. Can we truly say that we have been pursuing the goal of full employment if, when the national unemployment rate averaged as little as 3.5 percent in 1969, the unemployment rates for selected groups varied as widely as 2.1 percent and 27.9 percent? [17] Employment opportunities are distributed very unevenly by color, sex, age, occupation, and location. For example, the unemployment rate for nonwhites was 6.4 percent, compared to 3.1 percent for whites. The highest unemployment was among teenagers, 12.2 percent, and ran as high as 27.6 percent among nonwhite youths. Special problems of urban poverty areas are suggested by the 5.5 percent among all workers in those neighborhoods, and 7.2 percent for the nonwhite urban poor.

Economists frequently distinguish among three kinds of unemployment: frictional, structural, and that due to a deficiency of aggregate demand. Aggregative unemployment exists when the total demand for goods and services is not large enough, given wage rates and productivity, to reduce unemployment to what is considered to be the full-employment level, as during a business recession.

The other two types of unemployment—frictional and structural—can be distinguished if we elaborate the model of the labor market.[18] First we have to recognize that the national labor market is segmented, and that mobility among these various submarkets is less than perfect. The labor force can be classified in various ways—for example, by age, sex, color, occupation, industry, level of education, and geographical location.

Second, there can be wide differences in the ratio of job vacancies to unemployment in various labor submarkets.[19] A scarcity of skilled workers can exist along with an oversupply of unskilled laborers or there may be a shortage of vacancies for

[17] *Manpower Report of the President*, April, 1971, Statistical Appendix, and *Employment and Earnings*, February, 1972.

[18] The ensuing discussion is based in part on R. A. Gordon, "Some Macroeconomic Aspects of Manpower Policy," in *Manpower Programs in the Policy Mix* (Baltimore, Md.: Johns Hopkins Press, 1973).

[19] As pointed out elsewhere, it is misleading to define full employment in terms of an equality of vacancies and unemployment for the economy as a whole. See R. A. Gordon, *The Goal of Full Employment* (New York: Wiley, 1967), pp. 74, 88.

teenagers while vacancies exceed unemployment for prime-age (particularly white) males.

Finally, the level of unemployment depends on the frequency with which workers enter the state of unemployment (from layoffs, quits, and entry into the labor force) and the average time spent in search before a new job is found. Thus, the volume of unemployment is a product of labor turnover and average search time.

Against this background, we can distinguish the following kinds of frictional and structural unemployment:

1. Some "normal" level of frictional unemployment due to labor turnover, which is characteristic of the economy as a whole.

2. Differentially high frictional unemployment in some labor submarkets which is offset by relatively high wages or other attractions of the job, inducing workers not to move to other submarkets although they are able to do so. The classic case of such differentially high frictional unemployment is in the construction industry. Here the element of weather and the need to move from job to job generate a relatively large amount of frictional unemployment; but high wage rates tend to offset this disadvantage, and construction workers do not move into other industries even though they are able to do so.

3. To these types of frictional unemployment we may now add two components of "structural" unemployment:

   a. Differentially high frictional unemployment, with vacancies equal to or greater than unemployment, not offset by higher wages or other attractions of the job, but workers not able to move to other submarkets. Such differentially high frictional unemployment exists among migrant farm workers; but they are not compensated for this disadvantage, nor are they free to move into other occupations. The same situation may prevail in urban ghettoes. Unattractive, poorly paid jobs may be relatively plentiful, but job turnover is high, and so is the average level of unemployment. Because of both lack of skills and some degree of discrimination, these workers are not free to move to more attractive jobs.

b. Finally, we have the situation in which vacancies are less than unemployment in a particular sector of the labor market even though vacancies equal or exceed unemployment in the entire economy, again with no offsetting attractions, such as higher wages, and with workers unable to move to other sectors with lower unemployment rates.

Both these last two categories are structural in the sense that differentially high unemployment rates exist because of labor *immobility*; workers suffering from such unemployment are unable to move into other sectors in which unemployment rates are lower.

Frictional and structural unemployment help to determine the position of the Phillips curve.[20] Reducing any of the kinds of unemployment just described would tend to shift the Phillips curve to the left and thus permit a lower level of unemployment to be associated with a given rate of inflation.

Policies to cope with the structural aspects of unemployment have increased greatly in the United States in the last decade through manpower programs aimed at improving job opportunities for target populations. Little emphasis has been placed on reducing frictional unemployment in our first two categories. Since the beginning of the 1960s, a steadily widening array of

[20] Strictly speaking, these factors affect the position of the *long-run* Phillips curve. There is also a short-run Phillips relationship which reflects particularly developments in the relatively recent past. Not only may wage and price changes respond to changes in unemployment with a lag, but, even more important, the relation between wage changes and unemployment is affected by price expectations, which in turn depend on the past behavior of prices.

manpower programs has been authorized by Congress; federal expenditures on these programs have increased almost twentyfold. Today, the President is required to submit to Congress each year not only an *Economic Report*, concerned largely with our aggregative economic goals, but also a *Manpower Report*, which deals with the structural aspects of insuring that all "those able, willing, and seeking to work" can find jobs for which they are qualified.

Increasing concern with the structural dimensions of the unemployment problem implies a change in the nature of the welfare function guiding American policy-makers. Instead of simply writing as we did before

$$Z = f(U,\dot{P})$$

we should perhaps now write

$$Z = f(U,\dot{P},U_1,U_2, \ldots U_n)$$

where the U's with subscripts refer to unemployment rates for different sectors of the labor force. In effect, the aim of manpower policy is primarily to reduce the U for the groups with the highest unemployment rates; that is, to reduce structural unemployment. Hopefully also, by reducing such structural unemployment through manpower programs the Phillips curve also will shift to the left and permit a more satisfactory trade-off between unemployment and inflation, as was illustrated in Figure 1.

An effective manpower policy should aim at reducing *frictional* as well as structural unemployment. Most suggestions have to do with reducing search time, and substantial efforts have been made to improve the quality and to extend the services of the federal-state employment service. Clearly, much more still needs to be done. Specific manpower programs concerned with counseling, training, and remedial education also serve to reduce search time as well as the quit rate, and here again there is much room for further progress.

With respect to teenagers and young adults, the problem is

much more the frequency of job changes than the length of time spent between jobs. The public schools, particularly the high schools, have so far failed to affect turnover rates (and search time) for both graduates and dropouts through better counseling and closer contacts with the local employment service and local employers, more relevant vocational training, and stronger stimuli to students to absorb general education.

The contribution to total unemployment resulting from frequent job changes should not, however, be exaggerated. The great bulk of teenage unemployment (about 73 percent in 1968) consists of new entrants and reentrants into the labor force. More than half of these in 1968 wanted only temporary work.[21]

Among adult males, the unemployed are chiefly those who have lost their job and to a much lesser extent voluntary job leavers. Some fraction of the job losses resulted from inadequate qualifications and a mismatching of workers and jobs. The opportunities for reducing the turnover rate among such workers are heavily concentrated among young adults and underprivileged minority groups, among whom dissatisfaction with present jobs may be quite prevalent.[22]

Too little has been done about the seasonal component of frictional unemployment in the United States, compared to some other countries. It has been estimated that seasonal unemployment accounted for about one-fifth of total unemployment in 1969, or about 0.7 out of a total rate of 3.5 percent. The largest single contribution to seasonal unemployment in 1969 was made by those with no previous work experience; the second largest contribution was made by construction workers.[23]

Various estimates suggest that total frictional unemployment

[21] See Kathryn D. Hoyle, "Job Losers, Leavers, and Entrants—Report on the Unemployed," *Monthly Labor Review* (April, 1969), pp. 25, 27.

[22] There is a growing body of literature on the "dual labor market." For a useful introduction to and bibliography of this literature, see David M. Gordon, *Problems in Political Economy: An Urban Perspective* (Lexington, Mass.: Heath, 1971).

[23] This discussion of seasonal and frictional unemployment is based on my paper, "Some Macroeconomic Aspects of Manpower Policy," in *Manpower Programs in the Policy Mix.*

in the United States is in the neighborhood of 3 percent. A persistent effort by government, with the cooperation of employers, ought to be able to bring this figure down to around 2.5 percent during the 1970s. A third or more of this decline might come from a reduction in seasonal unemployment.

Let us return now to structural unemployment as we have defined this term.[24] Manpower programs in the United States have been chiefly concerned with reducing differentially high unemployment rates in particular labor submarkets. Manpower policy has sought to reduce structural unemployment by: (1) improving mobility between submarkets when such mobility is possible, as from unskilled to skilled occupations or from one geographical area to another; and (2) increasing and broadening the range of employment opportunities available to particular sectors of the labor force when the distinguishing features of these sectors cannot be eliminated, such as color or sex. It is possible to change someone's skill or the industry in which one works but not one's color or sex or (except through the gradual passage of time) one's age. For adults, also, the level of education or the effects of past environment cannot be easily altered.

The first of these methods of reducing structural unemployment involves moving workers from sectors with relatively high unemployment rates to sectors in which unemployment rates are lower. The second method involves making vacancies available to particular categories of the unemployed who were previously not eligible, for example, women, blacks, or those who could not pass specified tests.

This has been done in three ways, the most important of which is not usually thought of as a form of manpower policy—civil rights legislation and programs aimed at reducing job discrimination on the basis of color or sex. The other specific manpower policies have sought (1) to reduce unemployment in particular age-sex-color groups by improving mobility along some other dimensions of the labor force, as by improving skills

[24] The remainder of this section is taken from the paper cited in the preceding footnote.

(including such minimal skills as steady work habits), and (2) to induce employers to alter recruiting practices and job specifications so that members of particular age-sex groups and those with a relatively low level of education and skill can qualify for jobs for which they were not formerly eligible, even without any improvement in their occupational skills.

RETROSPECT AND PROSPECT

During the last ten to fifteen years, the Phillips curve seems to have shifted upward and to the right; the inflation-unemployment trade-off has worsened rather than improved, despite the billions spent on manpower programs.

As already noted, an important reason for this apparent upward shifting of the Phillips curve is the changed age-sex composition of the labor force—the increased importance of teenagers, young adults, and women in the labor force and the declining supply of prime-age males.[25] As a result of this changing composition of the labor force, the same unemployment rates for the different age-sex groups which in 1956 yielded an over-all unemployment rate of 4.1 percent would, with today's composition of the labor force, yield a national unemployment rate of about 4.5 percent.

Manpower policy thus far, after a decade of rapidly expanding programs, has done little either to shift the Phillips curve downward or to reduce the wide differentials in unemployment rates by age, sex, and color. Indeed, the dispersion of unemployment rates by age and sex has widened markedly since 1961.[26] The relative position of nonwhites has improved modestly in the last five years, but in 1971 the nonwhite unemploy-

---

[25] The short-run Phillips curve has also shifted upward because of the inflationary expectations generated by previous price increases. A major objective of the Nixon administration's wage and price controls has been to reduce these inflationary expectations.

[26] The result is due much more to the changed age composition of the labor force than to the increased participation rates of women.

ment rate was still nearly twice that of whites. And such comparisons ignore the significant decline in labor force participation rates among black males and the extent to which blacks (and other underprivileged minority groups) are still concentrated in relatively low paid and unattractive occupations (although there has been some improvement). Along other dimensions of the labor force there has been a decline in the dispersion of unemployment rates by occupation between the mid-fifties and the mid-sixties.[27]

Prospective changes in the composition of the supply of and demand for labor in the 1970s will continue to create challenges for manpower policy.[28] There will be significant changes in the age composition of the labor force: an increase in the relative number of twenty to twenty-four year olds which has already begun, an even more dramatic increase in the share of the labor force accounted for by men and women age twenty-five to thirty-four, and continued attrition in the share composed of workers thirty-five years of age and older.

Clearly manpower policy has a major task to perform in expediting this increased flow of young workers into steady jobs and to expedite their transfer and promotion into high-vacancy jobs typically manned by older workers. The more readily this change occurs, the less will be the inflationary implications of maintained full employment. This will require flexibility in recruiting, promotion, and personnel practices generally. A significantly younger labor force may also imply more labor turnover, and consequently somewhat higher frictional unemploy-

[27] For a study of unemployment dispersion along different dimensions of the labor force, see Gordon, *The Goal of Full Employment*, chaps. 5–6; also Charles C. Holt *et al.*, *Manpower Programs to Reduce Inflation and Unemployment*, Urban Institute Working Paper 350–439 (November, 1971). The latter source indicates that there has also been a decline in geographical dispersion of unemployment but does not confirm the decline in occupational dispersion that I have noted.

[28] The projections summarized in the following paragraphs are taken from Bureau of Labor Statistics, *The United States Economy in 1980: A Summary of B.L.S. Projections*, B.L.S. Bulletin 1673 (Washington, D.C.: Government Printing Office, 1970). For a somewhat more detailed treatment, see my paper, "Some Macroeconomic Aspects of Manpower Policy," previously cited.

ment, and perhaps greater intransigence in collective bargaining on the labor side.

The share of nonwhites in the labor force will expand somewhat in the 1970s. In contrast to whites, the black teenagers' share of the labor force will show some further increase. But, as in the case of whites, it is in the twenty-five to thirty-four age group that the supply of nonwhite workers, particularly men, will show the most rapid expansion. A less drastic but still marked decline will occur in the share of the labor force composed of nonwhite workers age thirty-five and over.

These prospective changes do not suggest any narrowing in the dispersion of unemployment rates by age, sex, and color; rather the contrary. To that extent, they increase the effort required of manpower policy and civil rights programs to shift the Phillips curve to the left, not to mention the more important issue of achieving a more equitable distribution of economic opportunity. Increased and job-specific educational efforts are called for. A higher level of education should help to offset, at least in part, the effect of demographic trends in widening the dispersion of unemployment rates by age, sex, and color.

Prospective changes in the composition of the demand of labor, by occupation and industry, have already received considerable attention in the literature, as suggested in another case study in this volume. There will continue to be a significant shifting in the pattern of employment toward white-collar occupations and service-producing industries. In the past, the labor force has been able to adjust to these changes. Unemployment dispersion by occupation, for example, remained substantially unchanged in the latter half of the sixties; if anything, there was a slight narrowing in the dispersion of unemployment rates by industry. The most serious problems of structural unemployment since the mid-fifties have arisen from changes on the supply side of the labor market rather than on the demand side.

The problem of ghetto unemployment suggests another significant change in the composition of demand to which an important segment of the labor supply has found it difficult to adjust. This involves the movement of industry to the suburbs, while a significant part of the urban labor supply, particularly blacks, remains concentrated in the central cities.[29] This is a problem that has been exacerbated by growing deficiencies in urban transportation and *de facto* discrimination in housing. It seems safe to predict that the problem will still be a serious one at the end of the 1970s.

The analysis of this case and a considerable body of supporting literature suggest that a large-scale and effective set of manpower programs *can* make some, hopefully not insignificant, contribution to improving the trade-off between unemployment and inflation. But that is as much as we can say.[30] In fact, because of structural changes, the relationship has actually worsened during the last decade or more, and manpower policy during the sixties was on too small and experimental a scale—and not sufficiently directed toward the problem of wage inflation—to have much offsetting effect.

While the emphasis will and should continue to be on providing greater equality of economic opportunity to the less privileged segments of the population, it is to be hoped that more attention than in the past will be paid to the ways in which an expanded manpower effort can contribute to reducing the inflationary pressures associated with the low over-all level of unemployment. This calls for a stronger effort to reduce particular labor scarcities, to stimulate more effective manpower planning by employers, to extend and improve the placement activities of the employment service, and so on. This is not to suggest, however, that manpower programs alone, on whatever scale,

[29] This problem received considerable attention in the 1971 *Manpower Report of the President*. See Chapter 3.

[30] For two strikingly contrasting views on this subject, see the papers by Robert Hall and by Charles Holt and his associates in Arthur M. Okun and George L. Perry, *Brookings Papers on Economic Activity*, 1971:3 (Washington, D.C.: The Brookings Institution, 1971).

are a sufficient supplement to monetary and fiscal policy to bring about a combination of unemployment rate and inflation levels that most Americans will find acceptable.

III. PLANNING FOR MENTAL HEALTH [31]

Mental illness has traditionally been viewed as a medical problem. However, treatment had never reached large segments of the population because of the extremely high cost of private treatment and the accepted practice of placing persons with deviant behavior in nontreatment, custodial care institutions. Only after World War II when Americans were jolted by the indisputable reports that hundreds of thousands of men had been rejected for military service as mentally unfit did this country face the fact of the pervasiveness of mental illness. Knowledge about treatment and prevention was still rather sketchy at that time, though it was believed that people recovered best when they were kept in the familiar surroundings of their communities, when they were not hospitalized, and when they did not become stigmatized by society for seeking professional help.

In 1963 the federal government initiated a process to re-examine existing practices in the field of mental health, reorient its direction and policy, and most important, devise a blueprint for a national strategy. The foundation for this new approach was to be community care, carried out through community mental-health centers.

The community care ideology developed from the growing realization that the mental hospital as it existed did much to isolate the patient from his community, to retard his skills, and, in general, to induce a level of disability above and beyond that resulting from the patient's condition . . . the new emphasis is on outpatient care

[31] This case was developed from a variety of sources, including Thomas Plaut, Benjamin Pasamanick, Linda Norris, and Rae McNamara.

and short periods of hospitalization when necessary. Moreover, new alternatives were urged which fell somewhere between total separation characterized by the mental hospitals in isolation from the community and outpatient care. If some form of institutional care is necessary, less radical alternatives than full-time hospitalization can be implemented . . . day hospitals, night hospitals, halfway houses, hostels, and so on. Moreover, an understanding of the importance of maintaining patients' skills and sense of activity led to added emphasis on vocational services, sheltered workshops, continuing employment while . . . in the hospital and the like. Finally, great emphasis has been given to the idea that patients should be kept in their home surroundings and that the necessary services should be provided to them and their families so that they can cope with the problems that arise.[32]

While treatment of mentally ill persons within the community and family structure was the primary purpose of the legislation, the centers were designed so that persons who were not mentally ill but were undergoing stress and needed help were also treated.

The centers also were to form a definite interface between the individual seeking help, other service agencies, and the community, thus allowing coordination of care and less duplication of effort. Another proposed goal was to provide guidance to various community caretakers who had numerous contacts and influence in helping individuals deal with their problems. Many of the center's activities were to be concerned with strengthening individual lives, but also included training and research.

The Community Mental Health Centers Act of 1963 which authorized federal funds of around $300,000,000 in construction and staffing grants administered by the National Institute of Mental Health (NIMH) provided for the development of these programs. NIMH was also given responsibility for devis-

[32] David Mechanic, *Mental Health and Social Policy* (Englewood Cliffs, N.J.: Prentice-Hall, 1969), p. 63.

ing regulations which would ensure that the intent of the act be carried out. The legislation put much needed support into the expansion of the mental-health service delivery system leading to a more comprehensive and coordinated program.

The act of 1963 and its subsequent amendments were based on the premises that mental illness and mental health are not problems of individuals, but are more meaningfully defined and viewed only in the context of society; care and treatment for those who are labeled "insane" is not the private function or responsibility of the family, but rather of society; society would benefit by helping dysfunctional members become at least somewhat productive. The act recognized the need for a national unified approach to mental health, and established funds for the construction and staffing of numerous community mental-health centers by matching federal funds with state and local funds.

BACKGROUND

In the fall of 1953, a conference on mental health was held in Washington, sponsored by the American Psychiatric Association and the American Medical Association. Dr. Kenneth Appel, president of the American Psychiatric Association, made a strong appeal for a nationwide survey of the problems of mental illness. As a result of that conference and the efforts by individual members of the two professional organizations, the Joint Commission on Mental Illness and Health was formed in 1954. The following year, Congress passed the Mental Health Study Act of 1955. Under this act, the surgeon general was authorized to make grants to one or more organizations, over a three-year period, for a "program of research into and study of our resources, methods, and practices for diagnosing, treating, caring for and rehabilitating the mentally ill. . . ." [33]

[33] Robert Connery, *The Politics of Mental Health* (New York and London: Columbia University Press, 1968), p. 30.

A grant of $250,000 was made early in 1956 to the Joint Commission on Mental Illness and Health, which by that time was organized and functioning. Thirty-six organizations were eventually represented on the joint commission, which defined its purpose as that of looking for new approaches to the problem of mental illness. On December 31, 1960, the final report of the joint commission, entitled *Action for Mental Health*, was submitted to Congress, the surgeon general, and the governors of the fifty states. The report, drawing heavily on position papers of NIMH, called for a comprehensive mental-health program integrated with the larger health-care system. It stressed the need for expansion of research, and better utilization of manpower, including the development of paraprofessionals and volunteers. It set as an objective the establishment of one full-time mental-health clinic for each population of 50,000 and urged training and consulting programs to take advantage of community resources. It is particularly notable that the joint commission report urged that large state mental hospitals should "be gradually and progressively converted into centers for the long-term and combined care of chronic diseases, including mental illness." [34] The only new hospital construction recommended was for intensive treatment centers of fewer than 1,000 beds.

The joint commission recommended that expenditures in the field of mental health be doubled in the next five years and tripled in the next ten. It also urged the federal government to assume a major part of the financial responsibility.

In November, 1961, President Kennedy appointed a Cabinet-level commission to analyze the joint commission's report in terms of action which would be appropriate for the federal government. As part of this process, some important political negotiations took place between the staff of the National Institute of Mental Health and the office of the President that undermined the objectives set forth by the joint commission. The

[34] *Ibid.*, p. 44.

National Institute of Mental Health, whose bureaucratic self-interests protected the accepted domain of the psychiatry profession, wanted a separate mental-health system. The President had a personal interest in establishing a separate program for mental retardation. Both objectives were realized in the final proposals recommended by the President to the Congress.

The work of the commission culminated in a message to Congress by President Kennedy on February 5, 1963. In his speech, President Kennedy asserted:

> . . . we must seek out the causes of mental illness and of mental retardation and eradicate them. . . . For prevention is far more desirable for all concerned. It is far more economical and it is far more likely to be successful. Prevention will require both selected specific programs directed especially at known causes, and the general strengthening of our fundamental community, social welfare, and educational programs which can do much to eliminate or correct the harsh environmental conditions which often are associated with mental retardation and mental illness.[35]

Thus the concerns and ideas of community mental-health proponents over the years were made part of national policy and were thus to become a reality throughout American society. The President called for action to "(1) find and eradicate the causes of mental illness and mental retardation; (2) strengthen the underlying resources of knowledge and necessary skilled manpower; and (3) strengthen and improve the programs and facilities for the mentally ill and mentally retarded."[36] The President also urged that federal money be used to stimulate state, local, and private action.

This was a shift from the joint commission's report in one respect. Whereas the joint commission had stressed the need for

---

[35] Franklin D. Chu and Skarland Trotter, *Nader Report on Community Mental Health Centers, Volume 1, The Mental Health Complex, Part I: Community Mental Health Centers* (unpublished manuscript of the Task Force Report on the National Institute of Mental Health), pp. 1–3.

[36] Connery, *The Politics of Mental Health*, p. 57.

community mental-health "clinics," the President referred to the need for "centers" which would provide more comprehensive services, and assure continuity of care, from diagnosis to cure, to rehabilitation, without the need to transfer to different institutions located in different communities. He asked Congress to authorize grants to states for construction of these centers, short-term grants for their initial staffing, and a relatively small sum for planning grants.

Legislation was prepared for Congress as a result of the President's message and a well-managed plan to ensure congressional approval was developed. Supportive testimony was given in congressional hearings by an impressive array of administrative officials and the representatives of professional organizations, all from the "in-group" which had been involved in the development of the policy. No hostile testimony was heard in Senate hearings. Questioning of the legislation was somewhat sharper in the House where two opposing views regarding staffing grants surfaced. One faction seemed to feel that federal assistance in supporting initial staffing of the mental-health centers was important to ensure that properly staffed programs could be implemented. Once started, the influx of patients and the transfer of state funds from other institutional facilities would make continued federal financial help unnecessary. On the other side, a group from the American Medical Association felt that if community mental-health centers received financial assistance from the federal government for staff salaries, the centers would become dependent on federal support. This continued input from a national source would hurt development of "community" ownership in the centers and would give the federal government too much opportunity to interfere with and control the medical personnel working in the centers. Conflict over the federal financial help for staffing and the amount of federal funds to be appropriated was the major issue of concern to the House.

The Senate bill was passed on May 27, 1963, by a vote of 72 to 1. The House version of the legislation, passed by a vote of

335 to 18 on September 10, 1963, provided for less funds than the Senate bill and for shorter periods, but most important, deleted the provision for initial staffing. A conference committee struck a compromise on the amount and duration of federal funds but the initial staffing provisions were left out of the final bill. Congress passed the new version of the legislation, and the President signed it on October 31, 1963. The Secretary of the Department of Health, Education, and Welfare was to issue regulations pertaining to the construction of mental-health centers which were to be applicable within six months to all states.

In January, 1965, only three days after his State of the Union address, President Johnson sent a special message to Congress, including a five-year program of grants to states for staffing community mental-health centers. This time the bill passed with little opposition, the only major question being the duration of the staffing grants.

Following this enactment, the community mental-health effort moved into a narrower political arena. Technical experts, professional groups in the mental-health field, bureaucrats, and managers at the federal and state levels were assigned the task of developing regulations that would interpret and make concrete the congressional language. For example, the essential services in the legislation were specified in the regulations. Similarly, the broad parameters of the community were specified in regulations in order to provide conditions that had to be met in order to be eligible for federal matching funds. So, in a very interesting fashion, central planning consisted of setting boundaries on the field, creating conditions under which a certain degree of local autonomy, local imagination, and local creativity could come into play.

ANALYSIS

The National Institute of Mental Health, created as a unit within the Public Health Service to be responsible for the re-

search, training, and service activities authorized by the National Mental Health Act of 1946, was to become one of the
strongest political forces in the community mental-health movement. From a budget of $6.3 million in 1948, NIMH grew to
administer a budget of $355.6 million in 1970, developing its
own research program and supporting research, training, and
community services by other individuals and organizations.

In 1962, Congress appropriated $4.2 million in matching
grants to states for the development of long-range and short-
range comprehensive community mental-health plans. Each
state was required to submit a "plan for planning" to NIMH,
and all states complied. It is interesting to note that the planning process was to some degree subverted by the passage the
following year of the Community Mental Health Centers Act.
The act provided only one year of construction money to be assigned to states, forcing state planning groups to focus their attention on the construction of community mental-health centers
instead of on the broad objectives of planning for mental-health
services and comprehensive programs. This crash effort induced mental-health practitioners into planning activities and
influenced the development of a complex bureaucracy of mental-
health administrators in the various states. The utilization of
highly skilled psychiatrists as administrators has continued
until today, and service delivery has suffered somewhat.

The intent of the Community Mental Health Centers Act of
1963 was not to subsidize the operating costs of mental hospitals, but rather, to stimulate new forms of community mental-
health activities. Each state was required to designate a mental-
health authority to receive grant-in-aid funds and to plan for
and govern their disbursement within the state. A state agency
restricted to jurisdiction over mental hospitals could not be so
designated.[37]

By refusing to allow states to name agencies solely responsible for mental hospitals as their mental-health authority, the

[37] *Ibid.*, p. 20.

National Mental Health Act of 1963 was instrumental in caus-
ing a division in many state programs, which in turn caused
philosophical and administrative conflicts, and sometimes led to
power struggles between mental-health administrators and proponents of the new community mental-health centers. One
study group reported: "The events of recent years . . . have
tended to draw a sharp line of demarcation between mental
health programs and mental hospital programs, with mental
health on one side and mental illness on the other, quite separate. . . . The mental health programs of health departments
. . . devote their special attention to what are called 'educational and preventive services,' and with few exceptions shy
away from having much, if anything, to do with the treatment
of mental illness." [38]

It is, therefore, not surprising that persons involved in the
state mental hospitals were prepared and did become one of the
strong political forces influencing the development and direction of community mental-health policy, and specifically, the
Community Mental Health Centers Act of 1963. Even today,
the state mental hospitals system is the principal method of care
for the mentally ill, both in terms of the number of patients
treated and the extent of financial support provided by the
state.

The substantive provisions and strategies of the Community
Mental Health Centers Act produced only a sketchy outline
when compared to the broad issues and objectives of the policy.
The act had the following major provisions:

a. Construction grants with matching state funds;
b. Staffing grants with matching state funds;
c. Comprehensive state plans which assess mental-health
needs and designate a single state agency as the mental-
health authority;
d. The provision of five essential services and comprehensiveness of care;

[38] *Ibid.*, p. 30.

e. The designation of catchment (geographical) areas to be served;
f. A reasonable volume of services to the indigent; and
g. Accessibility to poverty areas.

Basic to the provision of staffing and construction grants was the interaction of federal, state, and local government. Through NIMH, the federal government allocated certain percentages that ranged from one-third to two-thirds of the total construction costs, and percentages ranging from 75 percent for the first fifteen months to 30 percent for the fourth year to cover financing of initial staffing and operations expenses. Such budgeting is based on a matching funds concept in which the state/local governments would have to match the federal share. The federal portion was to act as "seed" money for a certain time period, at the end of which the funds would be withdrawn. The time would supposedly be long enough to allow for the development of economic resources to replace the federal share.

The use of matching funds has become increasingly important within the last twenty years. With federal funds as incentives, states were to initiate programs which are considered to be in the national interest. Since states have traditionally provided all funds going to mental-health services, most have had to allocate them to the extremely costly hospital systems, with an emphasis upon inpatient care. It was argued in the House Ways and Means Committee hearings that few states could afford the dramatic additional investment in new facilities and services necessary to make the national plan a reality.[39] The expenditures that many states had begun to make for outpatient clinics, bolstered by short-term federal outlays, would facilitate meeting projected needs within the foreseeable future.

Serious doubts about this premise were raised in the House hearings. Continuance of mental-health programs would become more and more dependent on the yearly input of this

[39] Joint Commission on Mental Illness and Health, *Action for Mental Health*, p. 279.

"seed" money.[40] At the time of enactment no assessment of whether state and local resources would be available had been undertaken. In fact, federal financing has been extended years beyond its original goal and there seems to be no indication that the areas which existing centers serve are able or willing to assume financial support once they are weaned from federal support.

In the third provision, comprehensive state plans, NIMH required that each state designate a single agency as its mental-health authority. This agency would be responsible for collecting mental illness and health data and inventorying present facilities, for dividing the state into service areas and assigning need priorities to each area, for anticipating possible locations for new center programs, and for setting construction standards. How these tasks were to be performed would be conceived in a written plan. Since the agency could not be the same one that administered the state mental hospital system, many states were forced to develop dual administrative structures, one dealing with the institutions and the other with the community. For others, this requirement was a boon because for the first time there was a possibility within the community sector of having some centralized planning and administration of an entire program area.

In order to receive funds, a center is required to offer five essential services: inpatient care, outpatient care, partial hospitalization, emergency care, and consultation and education. To be a comprehensive center, there should be five additional ones: diagnostic services, rehabilitative services, pre-care and after-care services, training, and research and evaluation. As originally envisioned, these services were thought to be creative and bold, definitely a step away from old models.

A further precedent-setting provision of the policy assigned a catchment area composed of a population of between 75,000 to 200,000 to be served by a community mental-health center.

[40] Hearings before the House Interstate Commerce Committee on HR 3689 and 2567, 88th Cong., 1st Sess., March 26, 27, and 28, 1967.

This concept, basic to the redirection which the policy proposes, is based on the feeling that planning and service delivery should be done on a regional level rather than within a county or municipality. In some large metropolitan areas, however, already divided by school districts, townships, and other equally arbitrary designations, application of this concept only added to the fragmentation of effort. The concept, if applied with consideration of individual community needs and organization instead of a rigidly held criterion (population), can be an effective measure of planning.

One of the most essential provisions of the policy is that concerning the delivery of services to the poor and the indigent. The regulations stipulate that:

> The facility will furnish below cost or without charge a reasonable volume of services to persons unable to pay therefore. As used in this paragraph, persons unable to pay therefore includes persons who are otherwise self-supporting, but unable to pay the full cost of needed services. . . . The requirements may be waived if the applicant demonstrates to the satisfaction of the state agency, subject to subsequent approval by the Surgeon General, that to furnish such service is not feasible financially.[41]

Built into the wording of this provision is the actual defeat of its purpose. By using the imprecise phrase "reasonable volume of services" and then by allowing even this to be waived, the regulation makes no substantive provision that obligates centers to serve the poor. Each center must decide for itself what a reasonable volume is, and most centers would have little difficulty proving that rendering any volume of services to the poor is a catastrophe financially. The provision discriminates both against individuals who are poor and against poverty areas.

In retrospect, the centers established after the 1963 act have not totally discriminated against the poor. But neither have the initial intended effects been pursued and realized. For example,

[41] Code of Federal Regulations, Title 42—Public Health, Part 54, 210(2) (January 1, 1971), p. 114.

a report by the Joint Information Service studying community mental-health centers found that "In one center to require inpatient care and be unable to pay for it was tantamount to being shipped off to the state hospital, regardless of diagnosis or history; this program in the year preceding our visit had provided inpatient treatment to only two persons unable to pay, and even these had been paid for by the welfare department." [42] Although this particular program may not be representative of the over-all attitude of community mental-health centers to the poor, other evidence, based on the negligible amount (2 to 3 percent) of total services provided to those on Medicare and Medicaid, confirms this finding. [43]

In Florida and California, centers deemed most important for serving poor people have had difficulty in being accepted for funding by NIMH. [44] The problem is common to other states and is an unintended side-effect of having had to prepare a plan, apply for funds, and show matching local and state funds within a very short time span. Rapid planning and matching funds means that an area must have resources on hand; poverty areas fall behind immediately and often are not served at all.

A final issue concerns services located in poverty areas. For such areas as much as 90 percent of the initial staffing cost could be paid for with federal funds. This strategy means that poverty areas need less resources to qualify for funds, and are more likely to be able to develop centers.

While the purposes of these provisions have grown out of underlying assumptions about state versus federal control of mental-health services, the substantive provisos leave much of this new service delivery system sketchy and barely outlined, with no explicit statements as to what the final program should

[42] Raymond Glasscote, *et al.*, eds., *The Community Mental Health Center: An Interim Appraisal* (Washington, D.C.: American Psychiatric Association, 1969), p. 12.
[43] U.S. Department of Health, Education, and Welfare, National Institute of Mental Health, "Descriptive Data on Federally Funded Community Mental Health Centers, 1971–72" (Survey and Reports Section, Biometry Branch, January, 1973), p. 11.
[44] Chu and Trotter, *Nader Report on Community Mental Health Centers*, pp. 11–40.

be. The federal government has parceled out its funding as a unifying base and has provided for a national plan but has not really engaged in national comprehensive planning. The provisions seem fragmented and are selectively used by states depending on their perception of their needs, their administration policies, and the realities of what will bring in the federal funds. There is lack of guidance concerning some requirements while others are too strictly regimented.

Although earlier sections of this analysis have suggested that mental health and mental illness are on a continuum, the methods for determining need in this area have been based on statistics of hospitalization or psychiatric treatment. Such data indicate usage of existing services, and depending on trends in population size, suggest future use of such services. Statistics on these population groups are important for anticipating needs if the centers in fact supplant state hospitals, or provide aftercare services to discharged patients, or take over some existing resources.

Estimation of unmet need—how many people need mental-health services and are not receiving them—is essential for the determination of impact and extent of the potential target populations. According to the Joint Commission on Mental Illness and Health, upwards of 16,000,000 Americans suffer some form of psychological disturbance which needs treatment.[45] Gurin, Veroff, and Feld, using a subjective survey in which individuals evaluated their own needs, found that one out of four Americans said that at some point in their lives they needed outside help with an emotional problem.[46] If the target population includes both those receiving mental-health services and those who need them, the task which the legislation was undertaking was mammoth. Clearly the proportions of the problem were not fully realized by the planners of the 1963 act.

[45] Joint Commission on Mental Illness and Health, *Action for Mental Health*, p. 4.

[46] G. Gurin, J. Veroff, S. Feld, *Americans View Their Mental Health* (New York: Basic Books, 1960).

One of the original intents of the policy was the gradual transfer of functions of state mental hospitals to community mental-health centers. It was assumed that state funds used in custodial care would be released, and therefore used to support this more innovative approach. It was further anticipated that public commitment, which for decades had been to the severely disabled, would be changed to commitment and concern for the estimated millions with lesser degrees of mental dysfunction.

In fact, these hopes have not materialized. Between 1966 and 1971, the number of state mental hospitals was actually increased, from 307 to 321. In addition, the hospital admission and readmission rates have increased from 802,216 to 836,326 during the same period.[47] Accompanying these figures is a further unanticipated fact: state expenditures have jumped 54 percent to over two billion dollars for the maintenance and operation of their mental hospitals.[48] These figures suggest that there has been little change in public commitment in the care of the mentally ill.

A third major intent of the policy was to initiate a new innovative mode of treatment which put to use scientific knowledge gained in the last several years. Hand in hand with the community health center structure went a new approach to diagnosis and treatment of mental illness in individuals. Use of this approach tested the authority of the practicing psychiatrists. What has been called the "medical model" was to be replaced by a new model which emphasized community factors. The medical model analyzes mental illnesses the same way physical diseases are diagnosed, locating the cause within the individual and prescribing appropriate treatment. The community model emphasizes the social and environmental dynamics involved in mental illnesses; it also tends to be more occupied with mental health rather than illness. Traditionally psychiatrists have been strong supporters of the medical model.

[47] Chu and Trotter, *Nader Report on Community Mental Health Centers*, pp. 11–28.
[48] R. Redich, "Maintenance Expenditures—State and County Mental Hospitals, 1955–71," National Institute of Mental Health Biometry Branch, June 30, 1972.

The effect of the program has been an endorsement of the medical model. This is easily seen by noting that four of the five essential services are based on the medical model and are far from innovative or bold: inpatient care, outpatient care, partial hospitalization, and twenty-four–hour emergency care. The requirement to offer inpatient services has led to a profound unintended effect: over half the centers now in operation were built as part of medical facilities, reinforcing the fact that those who already have some resources are at a definite advantage.[49] In addition, the psychiatric power structure has been strengthened and expanded. Eight out of ten directors of community mental-health clinics are psychiatrists, most of whom are untrained as administrators.[50] It appears that the new complex system of centers is developing a mental-health structure parallel to state mental hospitals.

The underlying rationale of mental-health policy was to provide federal seed money as incentive for state and local governments in such volume as to change their mental-health orientations. In fact, thus far only $477,000,000 has been spent for the entire program. This is less than the state of New York spends in one year for its mental-health program. As pointed out in the provisions, staffing and construction grants were originally time limited, and focused on decreasing use of federal funds as the programs progressed. Initially states were quite willing to take advantage of this opportunity—325 centers have been created throughout the fifty states. But it has become more and more difficult to withdraw federal support from such activities so that the original incentive funds have been applied to sustain fledgling centers. The construction grants have been expanded to emphasize poverty areas as well as to include building of centers designed for more specific target populations (alco-

[49] U.S. Department of Health, Education, and Welfare, "Progress Report: Community Mental Health Centers," Public Health Service, Health Services and Mental Health Administration (July, 1970).

[50] Chu and Trotter, *Nader Report on Community Mental Health Centers*, pp. 11–14.

holics, drug addicts). The controversial original staffing grants have also been extended.

The unintended effect of this policy, as pointed out in the Nader Report on Community Mental Health Centers, has been the creation of service monopolies.[51] This has happened because there can be funding for only one center in a catchment area. Nothing, except perhaps conscience, can ensure that the services will be administered equitably or that they will be of high quality.

Evaluation of the first ten years of this program points to a failure to move toward the original goals. State hospitals have not been supplanted; the medical model and psychiatric profession are thriving; services are not especially oriented toward the needs of the consumers; and the services remain inaccessible to large groups of people.

On the positive side, over 300 centers have been constructed. Some are striving to serve all the people in their catchment areas, in spite of the regulations. In addition, some provisions have been changed to bring the program more in keeping with its original intent: more service is going to poverty areas; no longer are psychiatrists required to be directors of centers; the catchment area criteria are less rigidly adhered to; and centers seem to be moving toward services which concentrate on consultation, education, as well as comprehensive care. The question becomes, was the original policy adequate? Much of the inadequacy was built into the legislative provisions and administrative regulations. In the last analysis, a policy is only as good as its means of implementation.

[51] *Ibid.*, pp. 11–15.

CHAPTER THREE

SOME ALTERNATE VIEWS OF CENTRALLY PLANNED CHANGE[1]

The case studies introduced in the previous chapter force a reconsideration of the definition of centralized planning with which this volume began. The areas of urbanization, employment, and health were chosen because they illustrate the complexity and interplay of social welfare objectives, the clash of value judgments, the ambiguity of definition and opposing technical appraisals which seem to characterize planned efforts to deal with social problems. But attempts at central planning for such diffuse social objectives bring out in sharp relief the limitations of rigid adherence to a logical formulation within the reality of American life. In fact, it is nearly impossible to discern all four elements of the definition advanced in Chapter 1 in any of the examples: national scope, institutionalized control of resources, a developmental process, and redistributive effects.

Planning was born out of the rationalism of the nineteenth century and its capacity to select single purposes for study by scientific means. With a single goal, the decision-maker or planner can enunciate his aims, define his problem, limit his attention to untangling cause and effect pathways from problems

[1] This chapter is based in part on a paper prepared by Robert Barre entitled "The Developing American Structure for Planning."

to solutions. The idea has only theoretical value for today's world. As pointed out in the case study of urbanization, most problems in American society are dependent upon one or more other objectives in society. Not surprisingly, social problems wash over into other areas in society. Employment level is linked to price fluctuation; the deterioration of the urban environment is related to population and economic growth; and our approach to mental health is constrained by the professional specialization throughout society. The social difficulties and the complexities of the twentieth century present scientific questions which are systemic in nature, which are not easy to reduce or to separate into manageable and manipulable components. When this interconnectedness of parts is recognized, extreme pessimism about any planning effort sets in. Partial planning efforts may have as disastrous results as the condition we are trying to remedy, as in urban affairs, or the expenditure of enormous energy and resources may not alter the underlying situation, as in the case of mental illness.

Finally the human and political aspects of social planning are at least as important as the practical feasibility of any large-scale planning. Social problems touch upon the most individualized and private areas of citizens' lives—where they will live, what they will eat, where they will turn when they are sick, what kind of a job they will hold, how their children will be educated. These are areas about which we are most jealous, most suspicious of intrusion into. No planner can predict how a citizen or group of citizens will react when he attempts to affect these personal areas of life. Similarly, the goods and services designed through planning are produced by formal organizations which display powerful reactions against any effort to modify their production. While such reactions may be understood, they are not easily controlled.

For these and for other reasons, it is not easy to find clear examples of American planning which fit our definition in which a decision center defines a specifiable goal, examines alternative approaches, selects one by logical analysis, and applies appropriate resources to achieve the desired end state which can be measured after a reasonable period of time. A number of other concepts about planning have been advanced. These can be perceived only dimly in the examples presented. Abstract planning methods are not usually explicitly spelled out as a rationale for governmental actions. But such ideas are worth reviewing briefly in the light of the case studies.

These alternate views can be distributed over a spectrum which runs from a minimal to a maximal belief in the capacity of government to consciously control or manage large-scale social problems. These alternatives can also be distributed according to the degree to which they are attached to the existing system of constraints rather than break away from such constraints. All views tend to account for two elements: a desire to put public actions into some kind of order or sequence through technical processes; and a recognition that diverging or antagonistic interests have to be harmonized through political processes.

VIEWS ABOUT PLANNING—MINIMALIST TO MAXIMALIST

Planning by Regulating

Government regulation involves the least departure from the traditional American belief in laissez-faire. The government is accepted as policeman for the common well-being when abuses in the marketplace operation become glaring. Antitrust legislation, regulation of the securities exchanges, inspecting restaurants for health purposes, licensing nursing homes and physicians are commonplace examples. This approach to planning is essentially negative. It assumes that nearly all social and economic needs can be met by the unhampered process of the open market, or through the unfettered processes of voluntary organizations.

It is often argued that such regulating measures do achieve positive results by indirection and with the least disruption of private choice-making. Licensing professional staff, in reducing charlatanry, in the long run benefits the health of a people. Regulating interest rates is intended to have widespread positive effects on employment or production rates.

This approach, however, does not usually provide for any public role in achieving positive results. Monopoly may be restrained but positive growth to produce more jobs or to redistribute the type of goods produced is not contemplated. The supply of physicians can be limited by imposing regulatory standards, but the supply is not positively increased nor is that supply allocated in socially productive ways. The spread of typhoid can be checked, but good health is not promoted, as through fluoridation of the water supply.

Although planning by regulating has been long supported as restricting the intrusion of government into what are considered to be private affairs, the scope and volume of regulatory constraints has grown to such an extent that vast public bureaucracies are now devoted to such essentially negative pursuits and equally vast private bureaucracies are required to help private organizations function within the negative constraints.

Planning by Resource Allocation

Resources, especially those of money, need to be allocated in any effort to achieve collective goals on the part of government or private organizations. Allocation procedures have come to be recognized as a specific, though limited, means of reconciling competing claims and demands on a social resource. Federal and state governments accumulate or control fiscal resources by various tax and excise means. Although these resources are accumulated to run the business of government, the use of such resources has evolved over the years to induce private enterprises or nonprofit organizations to undertake activities that achieve public objectives. The federal government has given grants or loans for the construction of facilities to private hospi-

tals and universities. Rural economic development and allevia-
tion of poverty can be met by tax funds to subsidize private or
corporate agricultural production, or to underwrite the growth
of farm cooperatives, or to retrain and resettle redundant farm
workers, or to make welfare payments. Unemployment on the
West Coast can be relieved by low cost loans or subsidy to large
aircraft companies to maintain production, by subsidy to small
businesses, support to ghetto economic development corporations, or funds for retraining and relocation programs.

Planning by resource allocation has the advantage of regulatory planning as a minimalist approach to governmental intervention. It places emphasis on the initiative of actors in the system, thus avoiding the conformity and deadening influence of
more centralized approaches. It goes beyond regulatory planning in that it allows government to pursue positive objectives
rather than simply control or avoid the excesses or inadvertent
harm generated by private actors in a market system.

However, resource allocation as the principal vehicle for
planning opens up certain abuses in the expenditure of social
resources. The actors who are to receive public allocations,
whether they be governmental bureaucracies or private enterprises, act as vested interests in the allocation process. They
first compete to define the nature of tax appropriations and the
purposes they are to serve. They also seek to persuade alloca-
tors that what they (the interest group) have been doing is exactly what the funds were appropriated for. University hospitals and poverty neighborhood health centers each seek to
persuade allocation officials that their efforts are the most effective means of achieving community health. A decision to return
care of the mentally ill from isolated state hospitals to the community sets off a jockeying for position on the part of psychiatric clinics, family service agencies, vocational rehabilitation services, and home nursing services, each arguing that the services
it renders are vital to such a new approach and should be supported.

Various producers represent not only alternative solutions but also political pressures with varying degrees of persuasiveness. Although it can be argued that government could make its allocation decision by some systematic planning process, the resource allocation approach lacks a broader planning capability and ends up characterized by a distribution among the contending or competing interest groups in a fashion which approximates their political power more than their capacity to relieve the situation.

A similar process takes place among private allocating organizations which seek to satisfy multiple claims by functional interest groups through some balanced allocation of whatever resources are raised by United Funds and other private philanthropies.

In sum, an attempt to plan through resource allocation usually ends up as a response mechanism by the holder of funds to pressures from competing interest groups.

Administrative Planning

Large governmental programs, created to deal with specific problems, generate their own dynamism for planning based on functions assigned to them as well as organizational objectives of their own. The Social Security Administration, established to assure security for the elderly in retirement, has become a major instrument for affecting poverty levels and the economy. The Department of Housing and Urban Development in affecting the supply of housing alters the character of the urban environment. The National Institute of Mental Health in executing the Community Mental Health Act reorganizes the delivery of social services at the community level. Such agencies are the vehicles by which public policy is executed, but they also acquire a quasi-independence for planning through their need to make operational decisions about the use of allocated resources.

The hierarchical organization allows these agencies to translate the general directives given them into a manageable set of actions through administrative procedures. This type of planning has no input into the goal selection at the outset, but through its efforts to fit agency resources, personnel interests, and the demands of patrons and clients into a program such planning shapes and reshapes the original intent of the effort. These actions are always colored by the desire to keep the agency alive. In such a limited construct for planning, the techniques of program planning and budgeting, benefit cost analysis, and Program Evaluation and Review Technique (PERT) programming find their greatest applicability. However, administrative planning is not necessarily narrow in effect. The Social Security Administration's decision to make vendor payments for old age recipients in nursing homes stoked the growth of a major new force in the health system, nursing homes as "an industry." Such decisions can be made as a reaction to a social problem deemed to be in the organization's arena of interest, or they can be made with the intent to achieve organizational aggrandizement. In either event, all of the characteristics of planning theory, as distinguished from administrative management, are applied within a framework clearly bounded by the conditions of the organization and its immediate environment. Planning is essentially "in-system" and incremental.

Such an approach does not provide for national planning in government. Various agencies and departments may develop planning units for their specific departmental purposes (administrative planning) but these represent refinements in the way in which government in an inclusive sense carries on its business. The sum total of the decisions taken by government at many levels constitutes the real way in which the thinking of individuals and of special interest groups becomes fused into the decisions made by a legislature or by an executive. Because the gestalt of these decisions expresses society's approach to dealing with its social needs, some more comprehensive framework for planning is needed.

Planning as Initiated Change

Central planning is often viewed as a set of actions designed to set in motion a sequence of events in some area of government or of a society which has a life of its own. The initiator is no longer in control. The changes brought about and results finally achieved cannot be determined. In this view, the interrelationships among organizations and associations and persons in modern society are so complex that control cannot be maintained over all interactions, nor is such control considered philosophically desirable. The objective is simply to jar loose the existing state of affairs in the hope that action, once begun, will produce some improvement over the existing situation.

Many recent efforts of the federal government are consistent with this approach. Rather than seeking to introduce a logical system, as we had done with Social Security in 1935, incentives such as matching funds and grants-in-aid have been offered to stimulate the state and local governments and voluntary and profit-making groups to come forward with their own proposals for coping with a given problem: decay of the inner city, poverty in the ghetto, drug addiction, juvenile delinquency, and mental illness. While a few general guidelines are laid down for granting the incentives, by and large the federal disbursing agency is free to accept whatever seems reasonable and not inconsistent with authorizing laws. The functioning program then is twice removed from the initiating planning body, the Congress.

A variation of this concept is found in the guided planning methods developed in France. National economic and social goals are developed in broad outline by governmental and quasi-public bodies. Then legal and financial incentives are made available to induce business, labor, and other functional groups in society to act in their own interest but in a mode consistent with broad societal aims.

Comprehensive Planning

In its extreme form, this approach implicitly embraces all aspects of modern society under at least the scrutiny of formal planning procedures. This approach places a high value upon formalized planning procedures for assessing conditions and for selecting preferred courses of action, rather than relying primarily upon the political interplay among interest groups. Even more, it seeks to identify rather broad social purposes and to bend the efforts of many disparate organizations to serve such purposes.

Comprehensive planning calls for mechanisms and authority which can cut across or can rise above the compartmentalized agencies and interests which deal with parts of a subject. Planning to reduce over-all unemployment requires simultaneous and coordinated control of inflation; manpower development; vocational training; selective programs for minority groups, handicapped or educationally ill-equipped groups; and provision of child-care facilities for working mothers. Comprehensive health planning requires a coordinated attack on facility construction and location; recruitment, training, and location of skilled personnel; health education; methods of financing and insurance practices; the structure of medical practice; improvement of income, housing, and nutrition for vulnerable populations; and so on.

While comprehensive planning tends to be more rational and more inclusive in its consideration of the various facets of a problem, it tends to be more removed from actual practice. Since comprehensive planning is relatively isolated from political pressures and day-to-day decisions, it is likely to have less influence on the accumulation of incremental decisions that often form the substance of planned change.

Planning as a Way of Thinking

Here the link between thinking and action is very nearly severed, although the need for action at some point in time is acknowledged. The thrust is on thinking out alternatives and their consequences, reflecting on the results if action were taken, and adjusting targets in the light of new information, through a constant cybernetic or feedback process. Planning is considered a learning process.

Rational effort is shielded from the exigencies of daily political pressure during the "thinking out" stage, but the results are then fed, by various means, into the political or decision centers. Reactions there provide a feedback which nourishes or enriches the next stage of thinking and planning. This view is compatible with the belief that planning departments should be established outside the daily operational flow of any organization. By such separation, planners are able, hopefully, to go beyond the current constraints imposed by institutional forms with a time frame longer than that usually permitted in day-by-day operations.

Planning as Futurism and Innovation

This approach to planning emphasizes the advancement of knowledge. It is assumed that over time this theoretical knowledge will become incorporated in public actions. One example of this approach is the work of those planners who concentrate on designing an idealized portrait for the future in which conditions are predicted and where end-states conceived are free of the social difficulties encountered today. While the blueprints for the future that emerge often seed and fertilize decisions, there is seldom a direct link between the futurist plan and action that is appropriate and feasible in the current environment. Scenarios for various ways in which a society can move from the unsatisfactory present to the more desirable future most often relate the way natural forces will play out events, rather than provide a guide for action.

The function of planners is seen primarily as a resource for innovative ideas. Goals are clearly expressed but they are planners' goals for planning, *sui generis*, so to speak. The goals of other decision-makers to whom planners are accountable and whose reactions they must be prepared to receive are not considered in this model of the planning process.

Planning as Government at Work

The final alternative way of looking at planning is almost a nonplanning view. It implies that all actions of government, by the legislature and by the executive, are planning because they represent the calculated response of our system of government whereby formal institutions come to grips with social problems. In this view, the Land Grant College Act and the Pacific Railway Acts of the nineteenth century were creative responses, through government, for meeting perceived needs of the time; and the antitrust legislation and workmen's protective laws of the early twentieth century, the New Deal actions of the 1930s, and the Great Society actions of the 1960s are all illustrations of central planning.

Although this view does not require a separate planning function, deliberation by government as it seeks to draft laws and to develop responses to social need is given priority. The approach eschews impulsive reaction to crisis through panic legislation. Interchanges between legislatures and constituencies and between executive agencies and the legislature will sort out and assess alternatives. This deliberation, however, can be developed out of a mosaic of unconnected decisions, each of which uses evidence, analysis, motives, and consultation in a different manner.

REQUISITES OF CENTRAL PLANNING

Clearly a universal conception about central planning has not yet emerged, at least not one to which a majority of those who engage in major planning activities can agree. The central dilemma centers on values deeply held in this society about the nature of government and values which are inharmonious, but just as ingrained in our culture, that revere technological improvement and efficiency of production and delivery. Modern man strikes a balance between these elements in his individual life, but the tenuous aggregation of daily decisions fails as the scale of problems extends beyond an individual life. So far we have found no workable synthesis of the goals of individual freedom and rational planning that can support the development of a discipline of planning or can form criteria for the decision-making of a planned organization.

Before taking up this issue in detail in the next chapter, certain requisites of centralized planning which must be considered, regardless of the mix of politics and rationality, need to be understood. These requisites are (1) structures for planning, (2) the scale of planning, and (3) the time frame within which planning takes place.

Available Structures for Planning

Structure, in the context of centralized planning, means a formalized arrangement for the planning function within the hierarchy of societal institutions. Such a structure is often envisaged as a haven or a powerful launching pad for the work of planners. More realistically, the formal structure is the recognized arena within which the technical and the political aspects of planning come together. Planning concepts that depend upon the political processes of negotiation and bargaining will thrive in a structure that assures opportunity for planners to engage in the hurly burly of political processes; when guiding concepts stress technical analysis, a structure which safeguards such analytic effort from external distraction will promote the planning process. Whatever the mix is to be, structure must provide for some interplay between these two facets of planning.

In recent years it has been popular to speak of the need for a planning arm of government. Some of the blame for the absence of visible planning to deal with social problems has been attributed to this absence of a national planning office. The

Council of Economic Advisors (CEA) has built a significant
foundation from which much of the technical competence to
deal with the economic direction of the nation has grown. With
its roots in a fairly specific purpose—the achievement of full
employment in the post–World War II world—the CEA has
continuously refined and furthered the use of economic tools
and economic concepts. While the CEA has not always found
the right solution to an economic problem, nor become the
dominant deciding force in the American economy, it has provided a focus around which the limitations as well as the powers of economic analysis can be continuously explored. The
results have been a higher level of informed opinion among executive and legislative decision-makers; alternative options have
been examined with greater rigor than before the establishment
of the council. The *relative* success of economic techniques,
when compared to approaches to other problems, has led to a
noticeable deference to economists' views even when seeking
new approaches to social (other than economic) problems. A
counterpart council of social advisors, drawing upon other social sciences for their technical competence, has been proposed.

This preoccupation with a single planning entity has ob-
scured the very substantial effectiveness of many administrative
centers in the national government which can, and sometimes
do, nourish the development of a comparable technique for
social planning. Although none of these centers claims sanction
to plan for the entire range of social need, they represent more
than the administration of narrow programs. Their personnel
have developed planning, information-assessing, and decision-
making techniques suitable for their subjects, and the actions of
their agencies do affect government's piecemeal intervention
into social planning. If a limited definition of planning is
adopted, that is, regulation of a laissez-faire society, the Interstate Commerce Commission, the Securities and Exchange
Commission, the Wage Price Control Boards, and the Food and
Drug Administration represent planning loci. If reduction of
metal illness and promotion of mental health is our objective,

the National Institute of Mental Health and the Health Services Administration constitute at least primitive structures for planning; and the Social Security Administration represents a potent resource for planning for economic security. There is even a Bureau of Innovation within the Medical Services Administration of the Social and Rehabilitation Service of the Department of Health, Education, and Welfare. The federally funded but independent Urban Institute, the Brookings Institution, or the Institute for Research on Poverty of the University of Wisconsin represent models for a more innovative and futuristic approach to the problems of poverty or urban development. This proliferation of such separate federal centers constitutes the elementary institutional framework for testing the application of planning methods and for the training of persons competent to function as planners at the level of national government.

In recent years, the executive office of the President, aided by the Office of Management and Budget, has become a focus for more comprehensive planning efforts to manage, to guide, and also to change the cumbersome federal apparatus. Many new ideas have germinated in these two offices that have subsequently been used to alter how we deal with poverty, with income maintenance, with racial tensions, or with urban decay. We know very little of the process out of which these ideas emerged. The way in which the executive office staff is organized is not fully disclosed, although we know its numbers have grown significantly. The products of its efforts in planning are exposed to wide public scrutiny as soon as action to implement ideas is initiated. The functioning of the Office of Management and Budget is better understood but its efforts at planning are limited by its basic obligation to monitor and control expenditures authorized by legislation, a commitment which hampers full examination of alternatives to a particular plan.

To match this evolution of planning within the executive branch, the Congress has begun to seek means of strengthening its own capacity to plan in ways which can maintain legislative parity with the executive branch of government. The General Accounting Office and the Congressional Reference Library have been turned to by legislators to consider their planning requirements and to help them define social problems and seek out appropriate legislative solutions.

Current Structural Limitations

Whether or not a single more comprehensive national planning center is established, *some* institutional structure that provides the environment essential for central planning in a technical sense is already in place. Before the addition of yet more structure is considered, we need to learn how best to use what presently exists.

Unfortunately these available structures do not provide the opportunity for even the most skilled and forceful administrator to perform the planning function. The legal basis for many governmental organizations lies in their charge to administer a specific program or exercise regulatory control over others. Thus, FHA is primarily concerned with mortgage finance and housing construction; its staff is not directly charged with deciding where housing should be located nor with weighing differential population claims upon a limited housing stock. The Office of Management and Budget is primarily concerned with controlling the federal budget. When it does act positively upon the selection of government programs for implementation, it is likely to do so on the basis of some benefit-cost analysis, accepting as given the ends laid down by enacting legislation. There is little leeway for exploring fallout effects of the action or for seeking out other and perhaps more promising means to achieve the same end. Little room exists for examining the interrelationships among a number of problems and a number of proposed interventions. Thus, the existing bodies are less accountable for *planning* than for controlling or administering.

The dominant tendency in planning theory has been to accept the structure of planning within the American context as given, and to discuss the functions that are viable within that structure. It may be more fruitful to begin with specifying which conception of planning is desired—the generation of new knowledge, or political commitment to institutional change, or some combination of the two. Once clarified, an appropriate planning structure can be built around this function.

The alternative planning models already outlined can be matched with the variety of planning structures discussed above. Three basic dimensions can be used in clarifying structural alternatives for locating the planning function:

1. Within government or outside of it,
2. Within the executive or the legislative branch,
3. Within a single planning unit or disaggregated throughout all sectoral units.

With the examples that are now in place, it should be possible to study empirically existing structures for planning to determine how they affect alternative planning functions. For example, the resource allocation and administrative planning models are essentially conserving in nature, accepting prevailing values. They emphasize working within established boundaries and sectors. Efficiency and management tools are heavily relied upon. The results are likely to be small-scale increments grafted onto the body of preexisting programs which are, in turn, biased by the nature of their staffing and constituencies. Such planning units are probably best located within operating agencies.

The initiated change and comprehensive models of planning probably must be located outside of operating agencies, although experimentation is needed to test better ways for feeding planning propositions into operations and back into planning. Such structures can increase the opportunity to think beyond the constraints of current operations and to affect the borderline relationships between now separate sectors. It can permit more attention to external consequences which accompany the actions of any single operating agency. On the other hand, such a location is limiting by its separation of the planning function from operational control and any influence over resource redistribution is problematical.

Regulatory planning is of necessity located outside of any one operating program but inside of government in that legal authority is required to function. It is usually negative and indirect in its capacity to influence the course of events since it is designed to control proscribed behaviors rather than to promote positive action.

Planning concerned with innovation and futurism is probably best located outside of government where there is greater freedom to think outside the framework of present program demands and the current value definitions reflected in political processes. The time horizon of such a unit is also less constricted by the electoral time clock. On the other hand, the unit's complete separation from government makes the short-term adoption of its views problematical, although its work may prepare the groundwork for a shift in views, values, and readiness to accept change that is more significant and long term.

A Sense of Scale

It is more useful to speak of the right scale or scope of a solution to a specific problem than it is to talk abstractly about large- or small-scale intervention. The usual discussion of scale in planning founders because the term is taken to mean an *a priori* belief that government should or should not undertake large and ambitious programs. The way we define each social problem implies its own proper scale of intervention. It is technically possible to fix the scale of intervention appropriate for a problem once it has been defined. Unemployment and poverty in Appalachia can be treated as a shortage of physicians and psychiatrists necessary to overcome the handicaps of poor health and lack of motivation, which call for intervention on a relatively modest scale. But if this poverty is seen as part of the shifting economic base and changing technology of America, then a much larger investment of energy and resources is inevitably required. Scale is not made up of financial resources alone but includes the amount of effort which any chosen intervention requires—effort on the part of planners, their sponsors, and other institutions. Lacking any validated typology of intervention/scale combinations, each planning effort calls for its own empirical assessment of the definition of the problem selected and the estimated effort and resources called for by each of several approaches under consideration. Four major combinations can be used as a guide to this sense of scale:

Large ends/large means
Large ends/small means
Small ends/large means
Small ends/small means

Prosecution of a major war, if it means the survival of a society, clearly calls for enormous effort, as the last two world wars attest. The abolishment of poverty has some of this dimension, as reflected in the experience of World War II when vast government pump priming and action led to the virtual disappearance of unemployment. Such large ends, that also require vast effort, depend upon the very widest consensus, which is most difficult to achieve. This leads to a search for some less intense effort toward the same end. For example, fiscal policy may have dramatic effect on unemployment, as reflected in the Kennedy tax cuts. On the other hand, efforts to reduce poverty among minority groups through manpower training may only succeed in shifting the burden of poverty to the aged or to youth. Such action represents the use of relatively modest effort to achieve quite large results. Building an economically viable new town cannot be successful, on available evidence, unless it is built with the economic requirements in mind for at least 200,000, and perhaps 500,000, population. New town building requires a sufficient scale of infrastructure in roads and water supply, in schools, in commercial and job-producing enterprises. If the scale of intervention is not sufficiently large, the results will be disastrous for the investor.

It is not at all clear that large-scale actions produce desired results. An intervention scale which is "wrong" for the problem is patently counter-productive. Enlarging highways into inner cities if such highways must end in narrow, nineteenth-century, inner-city roadways, or channeling large expenditures of money for medical care through the present fee-for-service system, may create more chaos than benefit.

The most highly prized combination is that in which relatively small effort produces very large results. Although examples are hard to come by, monetary and fiscal manipulation by government to affect the state of the economy may be one illustration.

The utility of such arguments depends on the extent to which the adherents of various planning models agree that there is an appropriate scale of effort suitable for a given task which government undertakes. Where this relationship is clearly established, a political decision to tackle a problem so defined might carry with it a more or less automatic consensus about the scale of intervention which is appropriate. If we can improve knowledge about the scale of effort required by planning intervention, and if planners with diverse philosophical views about their tasks can agree about such relationships, then controversy can be limited to whether or not a particular problem requires public action at all.

Respect for Timing

The temporal dimension of planning is often interpreted to mean political time—the likelihood that an effort will meet success in the face of a prevailing political configuration. Political time has to a degree a built-in cycle based on national and state elections. National planning must inevitably depend upon the reality that presidential elections take place every four years. Even if an incumbent is reelected, the period of campaigning introduces a lull in activity until the electoral outcome has been determined. And within that cycle there are the biennial congressional elections which may shift, less significantly, the thrust of a national administration within the four- or eight-year cycle of presidential control.

Such reality means that a four- to eight-year cycle seems an ironclad constraint on the time horizon for planning, although of course nonaction-oriented efforts of study, analysis, and education can go on for much longer periods of time.

However, time constraints also derive from the nature of the intervention in question. It is possible to estimate how long it takes to sink a physical foundation for a building, or a city, and this determines the timing of succeeding programs which depend upon that foundation. It seems to take about ten years within which to redevelop a major part of a built-up city after financing and legal authorizations have been acquired. It is roughly known how long it takes to produce certain kinds of professional personnel—doctors, teachers, and so forth. If plans require an increase in the number of such persons, the plan cycle must allow for the known time lapse for their preparation. It probably takes three to four years for fiscal or monetary acts to slightly move employment/inflation ratios. It takes some five to seven years for formal organizations to fully adopt and absorb any significant change in practices or behavior. Planning efforts which depend upon changes in institutional and in organizational behavior need to take such time scales into account.

These realities of time impose obvious demands on planning efforts of any kind. The constraints of timing are tyrannical in two respects. If the political process involved in the development of a given policy has a short fuse, the lack of long-term support for sustained work on social problems often frustrates execution. Attempts to deal with delinquency, poverty, and drug addiction were all abortive in this respect.

On the other hand, if a long lead time is needed to develop the necessary technology and operational programs, it is possible that the reality conditions to which the original effort was addressed will have changed. Urban renewal is a good example. Some of the program elements were designed around World War II but many were not operational until the late 1950s and early 1960s when disruptive forces of racial conflict, housing shortages, and high construction costs made the programs seem anachronistic. With the abandonment of entire neighborhoods in the 1970s, the discredited approaches of the fifties may once again be worth consideration. If the consensual goal at the inception had been assumption of governmental responsibility for changes occurring in major cities, and if planning had proceeded with the recognition that a generation would be necessary before major improvements could be established, the process might have developed more deliberately and we could have learned from the experience of interim steps.

It would be especially useful if the lead time could be lengthened for planning about more general problems. While we have become acutely aware that we lack a capacity to tackle so large a problem as the elimination of poverty, closing the gap between the poor and the rest of society does appear to be a realistic goal for our government. It is possible that such a goal could transcend the short-term cycle which presidential elections impose on the American process, much in the way that commitment to economic planning under the Full Employment Act has assured continuity of attention and orderly development of technical tools. If such a longer time frame were adopted successive failures of single programs, or incomplete success, need not then be fatal to a continuing effort. Rather, study of single program results could feed ideas for improvements and alterations back into the planning/action cycle in order to permit technical improvements while maintaining persistent effort.

A sustained planning effort over a longer period of time than is originally allowed for by the political time table requires a widespread consensus in society about the importance of the problem to be pursued. If such a consensus can be reached, it may be possible to institutionalize the technical process of planning for a sufficient time to permit development of appropriate techniques and to learn from the success and failure in their application.

Where such a consensus is lacking, both political and technical actions proceed by fits and starts. When the consensus is present but begins to waver, the planner is diverted into efforts to rebuild support, which shift the balance of his role from technical to political behavior.

Planners can learn to respect time without being tyrannized by it. Whatever belief system or technologic bias planners hold, the reality of time can be recognized and accepted by all. It seems less clear that the public is prepared to make adjustments in the time cycle of our constitutional system to permit effective long-range planning. Perhaps some better understanding of these tensions of the planners' job and the political context that has always surrounded it will come out of an examination of the issues of consensus and control in the next chapter.

CHAPTER FOUR

CONSENSUS
AND CONTROL

This book began with a model of centrally planned change as an approach to resolving our continuing, grave social problems, one to replace unsuccessful models proposed in the past. The model demanded four requisites: Centrally planned change must (1) be national in scope, (2) have sufficient resources to achieve goals, (3) yield developmental processes over time, and (4) be capable of redistributing resources.

At the outset we recognized that implementation of our model depended on a delicate blend of consensus and control. Centrally planned change requires control by centralized authority to provide direction for society, but in the American context such control always hinges on gaining consensus about these directions. In Chapter 3, other approaches reflecting various preferences about the nature of planning were reviewed as alternatives to the model we propose. While these alternative views vary in a number of ways, they all wrestle with the dilemma posed here—what is the relationship between consensus and control, between politics and planning, between aggregation of individual preferences and some form of technical rationality.

This chapter will focus on this dilemma which we see as the critical issue to be resolved in constructing any model of centrally planned change. Here we will examine alternative views about (1) the nature of consensus and its relationship to planning, (2) the nature of control and its relationship to consensus, and (3) the basis for a synthesis of these two forces.

ORIGINS OF THE DILEMMA

In one sense, the dilemma between consensus and control can be viewed as an inevitable fact of social life. Most discussions about the nature of planning are based on the recognition that any public or group decision, no matter how democratically arrived at, will vary in popularity from one subgroup within society to another. Any corporate action is likely to affect different parts of the body politic in various ways. Attempts to increase the popularity of a given course of action, to broaden consensus, inevitably limit the control exercised by centralized authority. In order to broaden consensus, those in power must bargain with groups that are unhappy with the proposed course of action, thus placing constraints on the ability of centers of power to act. Seen in this light, the dilemma between consensus and control is a normal feature of any society, though it may vary in intensity from one social arrangement to another.

There is, however, within the American political system a tradition that introduces a unique element, one that was tacitly accepted in the various planning stances reviewed in Chapter 3. Anchored in pluralism, our system accepts negotiation and bargaining as the primary means of meeting social goals. While recognizing the previous failures of incremental approaches that have developed out of the political realities of our system, we continue to reject attempts to replace these strategies with a rational, systematic approach based on technical means for decision-making. Our pluralistic society also appears to favor diffusion of power and authority in order to ensure that all segments of society have the opportunity to affect choices and priorities.

These political constraints have prevented long-term, large-scale commitments to the solution of any major social problem. Is the degree of control and delegation of authority necessary for central planning more unacceptable to us than the continuing existence of a serious and apparent problem in our society? Does central planning inevitably lead to the implementation of methods, both technical and political, that are possibly antithetical to the dominant values found in this society? In our minds we cannot imagine a public decision that was not openly arrived at with equal participation of all affected citizens; yet we expect to tap our great technological and organizational skill in solving problems. Is it possible for consensus and control to coexist?

With the exception of planning efforts during times of war, there is little evidence that central planning was ever proposed in this country, let alone implemented. Central planning implies some grand plan, the marshaling and channeling of resources, and developing mechanisms to assure their appropriate use. The few actual cases of central planning, for example, programs that grew out of the Merrill Act, the Department of Agriculture Act, the Railway Act, and the Homestead Act, entailed basically collecting resources and then making funds available within broad guidelines. It is not a question of whether we know how to plan, to mobilize resources in effective ways. We have demonstrated our technical capacities with the rigid system of planning evident in World Wars I and II. The question is not capability but rather a public acceptance of the necessity for that form of planning—planning that assumes that the scarce resources will be redistributed in a way that will maximize the planned for goal.

SOME BASES FOR EXPANDING CONSENSUS

How can such consensus arise or emerge? While the list is not exhaustive, a number of alternative bases can be identified. They serve to demonstrate that somewhere between the extremes of coercive totalitarianism on the one hand, and collectivized ideology on the other, realistic sources of popular support for needed societal guidance can be found.

Consciousness of Scarce Resources

Before society is willing to accept the personal costs—both individual and interest group costs—associated with centralized planning, it has to be convinced that resources are scarce. At this point in our history, except for the emerging energy crisis, the public is not so convinced. If this assumption is valid for society as a whole, it is equally valid for sectoral planning with respect to medical care, urban decay, or unemployment.

Interdependence between Planning and Politics

It is possible to deal with the problem of consensus for societal guidance by, in a sense, explaining it away. There are those who argue that planning and politics are two aspects of the same process and are synonymous with consensus-building. According to this view, planning is simply the injection of rational consideration into the political process. In this sense, consensus-building becomes a problem only when planning is divorced from politics. Central planning is not furthered solely by the development of technical instruments but rather is dependent on the politics of the society. Advances in planning technology are not going to solve problems of dissension.

Consensus through Conflict

A corollary of the above position views consensus as a synthesis between sharply opposed and even irreconcilable views. While those who see the interdependence of planning and politics tend to conceive of consensus as the meshing of disparate interests through negotiation and bargaining, those who see consensus as synthesis conceive of new interests being forged out of the clash of originally irreconcilable forces. From this vantage point, advocacy planning becomes the principal vehicle for consensus-building.

Development of New Constituencies

Another approach, still within the general framework of the political process as the seedbed for societal change, is the building of consensus for change through the creation of new constituencies. This approach is based on the assumption that those individuals or groups who might benefit from a change from the present social arrangements are not reflected in the prevailing consensus because the majority coalition has either not identified them or refuses to acknowledge their voice. Individuals outside the decision-making process often are not aware of the concerns and desires they hold in common. The planner, when he speaks for those without such a voice or facilitates their entry into the political process, expands the basis of consensus for change through the creation of new constituencies.

Consensus through Social Criticism

Finally, some argue that, under certain conditions, planning carried on outside the political process is the only way to build a consensus for change. This is analogous to the biblical distinction between the priest and the prophet. Prophetic planning, it is argued, is free of the constraints imposed by the political process and therefore is able to conceive a wider range of alternatives, and to be attuned to a long time perspective. New consensuses may emerge when the perspectives resulting from "detached planning" conflict with those resulting from planning within the political process.

Consensus then is the foundation for any shift toward central planning, and yet consensus eludes us. Except in the case of natural energy, we cannot yet agree that resources are diminishing so rapidly that resource allocation is necessary. If consensus is achieved, its permanence can never be assumed. For example, in Sweden, as the government reached its goal of full employment, efforts were directed to reducing income differentials. As the Swedish government has made progress on the distributional question, the previously established consensus began to break up. It was inevitable. Consensus is not only elusive, it is fluid. Consensus-building is a continuing process. As decisions are implemented after reaching a consensus, new circumstances are created that can require new consensuses.

COMMUNITY MENTAL HEALTH—WHOSE CONSENSUS?

The case study of mental-health planning specifically addressed the issue of what constitutes consensus and is illustrative of this country's history of attempts at planning. Research and expertise were brought to bear on a social problem through the work of the Joint Commission on Mental Illness and Health. As the recommendations of the commission were channeled into the decision process, the primary intent, creating a comprehensive health-care system, disintegrated in the face of a combination of bureaucratic interests and professional forces whose concern was to protect the status quo.

The legislation enacted by Congress in the early 1960s channeled funds to communities under very broad rubrics which could easily be diverted to the interests of the providers. In fact, there was very little attempt to restructure the mental-health system. Each particular profession pursuing its own self-interest offered almost insurmountable resistance to any serious coordination of services. Our system is basically provider-oriented, and only governmental intervention on a much stronger level will effect the kind of change required to establish a well-functioning health-care delivery system.

And yet, there is little likelihood that this dimension of federal authority or control would be allowed at this time. In the mental-health field there was a high degree of consensus resulting in specific legislation. To achieve this consensus, however, concessions had to be made. The question—one that continually plagues proponents of central planning—is whether these concessions will invariably result in federal control too weak to deal with the problem undertaken.

Because consensus may undermine goals, any apparent consensus should be examined critically. In the mental-health case, was the consensus achieved appropriate? Was it sufficient? The providers in the mental-health field apparently reached consensus that the federal government should become more involved. They also agreed that the involvement should be primarily financial and not structural. Congress achieved a consensus after deliberating over a series of proposals that were offered by the professional groups. A different consensus might have been achieved if other constituencies had been identified and additional alternatives generated. Friction over real alternative plans could possibly have tempered the strong voice of the various vested interests. If the mental-health subsystem is to be changed, and if this requires stronger federal involvement, consensus for this must come from outside the established mental-health structure.

CONTROL AND AUTHORITY

In our introductory discussion of central planning we proposed that authority be assigned to specific public structures, with control over resources to achieve some desirable end. The question is not whether there should be authority but rather how much, for what ends, for how long, and by whom.

The Defense Department is a possible example of a central planning body meeting our criteria. It has relatively free authority to work out alternative programs, to acquire resources, and to implement strategies with little political accountability. A more appropriate example is the federal highway program, which has authority to gather resources through the gasoline tax in the highway trust fund, establish standards in conjunction with state highway officials, and map and implement highway systems nationally.

These represent examples in varying degrees of control by a centralized authority of resources essential to achieve a national objective. It is not necessarily government as the single agent or provider, as in the case of nationalized industry and the national health service in Great Britain, though this specter usually causes Americans to reject all types of central planning. Within the concept of central planning is the assumption that a laissez-faire policy is indefensible and that government has power not just to intervene when the market institutions falter but also to shape, implement, and monitor activity. This implies the imposition of power on a malfunctioning system, such as the health-care system, forcing it to comply with certain standards.

The achievement of public or social goals requires, at some point in time, a decision by selected individuals who have the power to enforce it. For many, this assumption of power can only mean tyranny. Others argue that there will always be tyranny, whether exercised by government or private entrepreneurs. The real estate market in which individual developers exercise power over their own land parcels constitutes a tyranny in the aggregate over urban development. The real choice is which form is more acceptable: conscious, rational tyranny or a blind, private interest tyranny? Each case is overstated. Something between these poles is closer to reality. The planner stands at the edge of a moving crowd seeking to influence its progress and to change its pattern slightly. Of course, in order to accomplish this objective he has to know how the crowd behaves, what it wants, where it has been, and where it would like to go.

This form of central planning exists in Great Britain. Government, unlike that of the United States, has the right to reject any development which it considers contrary to the rational allocation of public goods. Central planning ultimately is concerned with the changing of institutions to achieve clearly stated goals arrived at through some consensus-forming mechanisms.

If government and planning were synonymous terms, the issue would be argued in political terms alone. Since, however, we are attempting to isolate distinctively centralized planning activities from the over-all operations of government, we need to consider the amount of authority and control which may be delegated by government to planning organizations and to professional planners. Once such authority is delegated we must recognize the influence on the planners of the knowledge that this authority can as easily be withdrawn, or that, at a minimum, their program for action will be reviewed by and will need the sanction of society or its political representatives.

The alternative views of centralized planning outlined in Chapter 3 suggest a variety of forms for the delegation of authority and control to the planning function. The most concentrated form of control is found in administrative planning. Here control over all phases of activity is lodged in a centralized authority. Administrative planning implies direct supervision over the design and execution of a planned set of activities.

In contrast, less stringent forms of control are reflected in regulatory and comprehensive planning. Here control rests in a set of rules by which individuals must guide their actions. Considerably more initiative and autonomy is provided the actors in such a system.

And finally, control may be reflected in the incentives offered by a centralized authority to induce actors into conformity with a plan. A minimal amount of constraint is exercised, since actors are under no obligation to accept such inducements. This form of control can be used either in allocation planning or comprehensive planning. To the extent that information about future conditions is an inducement, innovative planning can be said to embody this form of control.

It should be obvious that the form of control exercised has considerable implications for consensus. The more specific and pervasive the form of control, the more likely dissension will be generated. Presumably control in the form of inducements would be accompanied by the greatest amount of consensus in a system.

The amount and kind of control which will be exercised by central authority depends in large part on the culture of a given society, and reflected in the historical development of trust between a people and their government. It is generally accepted that in Great Britain there is more trust in the fairness of governmental action than there is in the United States. In the last analysis, faith in the legitimacy and good intention of government will determine in large part the balance struck between consensus and control.

A SYNTHESIS

The reason that many programs of national planning do not build in more centralized control is that the planners recognize that it would never be publicly acceptable. Approval for the plan and appropriations to support the plan require consensus. The skill of the planner then is one of optimizing both elements.

It is our view that optimization occurs when the planning and political process are seen as one. It has been traditional to view these two processes as independent. In actual fact, politics is rational in the sense that elected officials seek the most efficient means of bringing about the closest approximation of the goals or values which they represent. Injecting analytical power and relevant evidence into that process will achieve the best balance between consensus and control in central planning. In Great Britain the "public inquiry" is used in the planning process to meld the development goals derived by planners with the values and perspectives of relevant publics. In this country the processes of Congress, the public hearing, and the investigation serve similar purposes.

Central planning must incorporate procedures which enable us to choose purposes that best reflect values and then to use analytic techniques to develop specific strategies to meet these goals. The planning process is concerned with procedures of inquiry and analysis that bring together individuals and interest groups to formulate policies with some sense of commitment.

If planning is a long and tedious process of information-building, why should we expect the public to make judgments more quickly? Perhaps they, too, should participate in the learning process. In the strategies described in the following chapters—use of market mechanisms and decentralization—the public most affected by the planning is built into the planning process.

CHAPTER FIVE

PLANNING WITHIN A DECENTRALIZED FRAMEWORK[1]

Two concepts of planning have been proposed to resolve the dilemma of consensus and control inherent in alternatives to centrally planned change. One is decentralization of power and/or authority so that public actions are more consistent with the needs and desires of particular public constituencies. The other model, much favored by economists, involves using market mechanisms to provide public goods and services and to grant the consumer the power to select his individual preference. Decentralization as a concept of planning will be examined in this chapter in the context of three cases. One is the theoretical model of government decentralization proposed by Charles Tiebout. A second case is the worker self-management system in Yugoslavia. The experimental metropolitan governance of the Greater London Council, a two-tier form of government, will be described as the third case. The issues and details of these cases are simplified here to highlight issues in decentralization.

THE CONCEPT OF DECENTRALIZATION

In the shifting sands of governmental reform, code words are traced, become the focus of all attention, and then are washed

[1] This chapter is based in part on a paper entitled "Decentralization: A Challenge to Planning and Governmental Organization," prepared by John W. Dyckman, University of California, Berkeley.

away completely by new sentiments. One of these words which has persisted longer than most is *decentralization*. Of all the functions of government, the one least conducive to decentralization is planning, for planning is centralist even in its theoretical form. It emphasizes coordination—which as commonly practiced means appropriation of powers by a superior authority—and stresses comprehensiveness, or the system-wide outlook. Some writers on planning have linked the planning function to the cortical function in the human body, sorting and decoding messages and converting them into control directives. Given this background, facilitation of the planning function makes perhaps the weakest case for decentralization. Would the effective decentralization of many governmental functions crack the planners' crystal ball? What would be the guiding principles of planning under a decentralized structure? Can the planning function itself be decentralized significantly?

The term *decentralization*, as it is used here, distinguishes between the structural concept of spatial or territorial decentralization of the bureaucracy and the political concept of citizen access to decision-making. The first task is that of finding the right territorial domain for bureaucratic decision, and the second more ambitious task is one of restructuring the decision modes themselves, so as to open them to the affected parties in the society. These sets of considerations intersect, but they are conceptually different processes, with different practical consequences. For our purposes the territorial bases of decentralization will be separated from the idea of decentralization as devolution-of-government-powers, or the access question. In some formulations, such as that of Tiebout, the spatial organization of public activities is made the cornerstone of the access problem. But decentralization can also be thought of as applying to the distribution of powers without regard to place or governmental spatial units. This is consistent with the historic question of devolution of powers, political and economic. In its purest form, decentralization realizes the anarchist objective and the Marxian dream of the withering away of the state.

Decentralization can be thought of as just another expression of the issue of individual freedom versus social control. But however dated, the concept of decentralization has special immediacy for our period when there is a growing radical demand for direct participatory democracy. This political sentiment is fed by many streams arising from varied ideologies. It is a mistake, however, to see in it a rebirth of populism, for the setting and culture of politics is too far removed from those roots. Nor will the movement toward local control comfort many statist Marxists, despite the fact, as Henri Lefebvre says, that "We hardly need to show that Marx's radical criticism of political philosophy, the state, and bureaucracy . . . implies the objective of revolutionary praxis, namely, democratic self-management, without bureaucracy or state." [2]

Contemporary conservative theory proposes territorial and administrative decentralization. The spatial decentralization package is able to envisage administrative and even political measures but stops short of the drastic reorganization that would abolish the state. It is consistent both with the spatial foundations built into the American federal system and the distrust of centralized power embedded in our Constitution. As an example of this line of thought, the Advisory Committee on Intergovernmental Relations, following Henry Schmandt's work,[3] speaks of *territorial decentralization*, including the dispersal of the delivery of local facilities to bring government physically closer to the people and to facilitate the expression of resident needs and preferences; *administrative decentralization*, or devolution of administration of certain public services to neighborhood areas with delegation of decision-making authority, discretionary power, and program authority to subordinate officials; and *political decentralization*, involving efforts of local officials to distribute political power and policy-making authority

[2] Henri Lefebvre, *The Sociology of Marx* (New York: Pantheon Books, 1968), p. 148.
[3] Henry J. Schmandt, "Decentralization: A Structural Imperative," in *Neighborhood Control in the 1970s: Politics, Administration and Citizen Participation*, ed. H. George Frederickson (New York: Chandler, 1973), pp. 17–35.

through the creation of new, autonomous subunit governments.[4]

This type of decentralization can be seen as an effort to impose a finer grain on spatial organization. It implies sharing of
powers with a pluralism of subcenters, and participation of citizens at the neighborhood level, close to the roots. But it does
not eliminate the problem of how to aggregate diverse interests;
it simply assumes that interests are more homogeneous at the
neighborhood, or small unit, level than at the state or national
level. One virtue of the Tiebout model, and of some of the
work which has followed it, is the basis for aggregation provided in the model through the self-selection of small units of
government by individuals. The Yugoslav worker self-
management system also provides a basis for interest aggregation in the form of a common interest, the working organization. As we shall see, however, neither of these systems is able
to organize all the functions of the state with which planning
deals in a wholly decentralized manner.

The Tiebout Approach

What we have been calling the "Tiebout approach" is actually
an incomplete line of argument elaborated in various aspects by
Charles Tiebout and others in a series of papers.[5] It is interesting to note in retrospect that initially Tiebout undertook to
address the historic problem of the analysis of public goods described by Musgrave and others, and subsequently was led to a
theory of decentralization.

The Tiebout model can be summarized as follows. Each metropolitan area has a variety of local governmental jurisdictions

[4] Advisory Committee on Intergovernmental Relations, *The New Grass Roots Government?* Washington, D.C. (January, 1972), p. 3.

[5] Charles Tiebout, "A Pure Theory of Local Expenditure," *Journal of Political Economy,* 64 (October, 1956), pp. 416–424, and "An Economic Theory of Fiscal Decentralization," *Public Finances, Needs, Sources and Utilization* (Princeton, N.J.: Princeton University Press for the National Bureau of Economic Research, 1961).

(the central city and its surrounding suburbs). Each jurisdiction provides a particular package of public goods and services: schools, health and welfare services, parks, cultural institutions, fire and police protection, and so on. Each jurisdiction has a tax package (property, sales, income, use taxes) to pay for such services. It is a commonplace observation that in any metropolitan area a considerable variation exists in the particular package of services provided by the respective local governmental jurisdictions. Some spend more on schools while others emphasize welfare services or cultural institutions. Similarly there is considerable variation in the amount as well as type of taxes levied to pay for such services. The Tiebout model treats the metropolitan area as a market; each of the local governmental jurisdictions is a producer offering different packages of public expenditures and taxes. The model assumes that there is a sufficient number of such jurisdictions to provide consumer choice. Each consumer, a household, reveals its preferences for local public goods through moving into a particular community where the differentiated tax/expenditure package is best adapted to its wants. "Note that revealed preferences are not detected or exchanged voluntarily by use of prices for individual public goods, but rather by what may be described as a single, collective price for a *package* of public goods . . . in the form of a local property tax payment." [6]

Tiebout sought to resolve the problem of differing preferences for the products of the state through a market-based mechanism of social organization, local government. In short, decentralization would be accomplished through the offering of distinctive community packages among which perfectly mobile consumers would choose. Tiebout thereby assumed away the problem of diversity of interest within the community which plagues most decentralization proposals. The model theorizes that individuals are thus forced to reveal preferences for public

[6] Statement of Richard P. Burton before the Joint Economic Committee of the U.S. Congress, October 15, 1970.

goods and services, and that their interests will be accommodated within a group of unique local governments.

Critics were quick to respond to the tenuous strength of the model, criticizing the artificiality of assumptions, particularly those of perfect mobility and the desire of consumers to choose homogeneous communities based on preferences for public goods and services. From a planning standpoint, other criticisms were even more serious. In particular, the existence of externalities *between* communities, spillovers and spill-ins, was entirely absent in the model.[7] Communities faced with the spillover of some of its supply of public goods to persons outside the communities would tend to undersupply those goods, and the addition of spill-ins raises the specter of possible oversupply as well. This, combined with the existence of privately produced externalities—air and water pollution, solid and liquid waste discharge, traffic congestion, and so on—points dramatically not to the breakdown but to the limitations of the local, polycentric "market mechanism" to respond to metropolitan-wide public service requirements. Recognizing the existence of these conditions has led metropolitan planners to argue for the creation of larger planning units within which all influences would be contained.

Certainly, as Margolis has noted,[8] Tiebout failed to specify the political processes by which the government policies were to be formed. Political mechanisms are left out of his argument. His model is dependent on the assumption that consumers would be able to find others with the same preferences and the same ability and willingness to pay for satisfying them, and demands of those groups would cause communities to be formed. Without this assumption, the theory would lead to communities of single persons. It appears, therefore, that Tiebout had in mind some social processes through which people

[7] Alan Williams, "The Optimal Provision of Public Goods in a System of Local Government," *Journal of Political Economy*, 74 (February, 1966), pp. 18–33.

[8] Julius Margolis, "The Demand for Public Services," *Issues in Urban Economics*, eds. H. Perloff and L. Wingo (Baltimore, Md.: Johns Hopkins Press, 1968).

of like preferences would come together, though he is not explicit on this point. (Buchanan has dealt with similar processes in his theory of clubs.) [9]

Furthermore, Tiebout's world is one of "compartmentalized equals," as Burton puts it. By treating business and industrial users in the same manner as residential households, Tiebout appears to have restricted his model to dormitory suburbs. More important, however, the assumption of homogeneous (at least in terms of consumption of public goods) households implies approximate unanimity in tastes, age, incomes, and wealth.

Despite these objections, the Tiebout model delineates the potential of local government to achieve one of the prime purposes of the decentralization movement, responsiveness of government to local preferences. Since Tiebout's model allows the single-person community, however, it can degenerate into the fantasy world of each person as his own municipal government unless, as he put it, "some sociological variable is introduced." Looked at another way, Tiebout's model did not solve the contradiction between the social aggregation of people in communities and the requirement of individual value economics that individuals get the public goods they prefer when their preferences are revealed. Even homogeneous preferences, when aggregated into communal units, require some procedures for collective decision-making.

Nevertheless, the same market mechanisms on which this model relies have some force in the American context. In a 1957 paper, for example, Margolis described and classified functionally distinct types of communities in the San Francisco metropolitan region.[10] Without directly testing the Tiebout hypothesis, his study lends some credence to the view that households do a certain amount of "voting with their feet" for packages of public goods.

[9] James M. Buchanan, "An Economic Theory of Clubs," *Economica*, 32 (February, 1965), pp. 1–14.

[10] Julius Margolis, "Municipal Fiscal Structure in a Metropolitan Region," *Journal of Political Economy*, 65 (June, 1957), pp. 225–236.

A more recent and direct empirical test of the Tiebout argument was undertaken by Oates.[11] He hypothesized that local government will choose the tax/benefit package which maximizes the value of local property. This proposition was tested by analyzing the relationship between property values, property tax rates, and local expenditures for public education in a sample of fifty-three New Jersey suburban communities. His finding is consistent with the Tiebout model in which rational consumers weigh the benefits from local public services against the cost of their tax liability in choosing a community of residence.

Warren examined the model of a market for municipal services in a metropolitan context in which control (and purchase of public goods) was decentralized while production was centralized.[12] This latter allowed both economies of scale in production and further decentralization. Warren proposed a competitive market for the centrally provided services as an answer to the intercommunity spillovers, a system which would not require the corollary of centralized decision-making. Other arguments along this line have been offered by Tiebout and Houston.[13]

Essentially these models substitute market processes for political processes. They treat governments as if they were firms. They are relatively silent on questions of who controls the firm. In this they are very different from the main thrust of decentralization proposals of groups like the Advisory Commission on Intergovernmental Relations, which seeks to modify "normal bureaucratic decision-making, personnel, and accountability practices." Underlying the Tiebout-type models is the

[11] Wallace E. Oates, "The Effects of Property Taxes and Local Public Spending on Property Values: An Empirical Study of Tax Capitalization and the Tiebout Hypothesis," *Journal of Political Economy*, 77 (November–December, 1969), pp. 957–971.

[12] Robert Warren, "A Municipal Services Market Model of Metropolitan Organization," *Journal of the American Institute of Planners*, 30 (August, 1964), pp. 193–204.

[13] Charles Tiebout and D. B. Houston, "Metropolitan Finance Reconsidered: Budget Functions and Multilevel Governments," *Review of Economics and Statistics*, 44 (November, 1962), pp. 412–417.

belief that loosely formed groups acting as consumers can force the responsiveness and accountability of the supplier bureaucracies. Market control is substituted for political control.

Tiebout's model has the virtue, however casually defended, of recognizing the importance of homogeneity in consumer units to the argument for allowing small local governments to act as the purchasing units. The issue is confronted from a perspective quite different from that of many advocates of neighborhood governments, neighborhood corporations, and local community control of public functions.[14] These proponents of decentralization seem to be seeking local control as an end in itself without considering whether there is enough common interest within an urban neighborhood to make the power of the locality effective.

YUGOSLAV WORKER SELF-MANAGEMENT

In Yugoslavia a system in which national welfare is sought through the decentralized action of relatively small subunits is in effect. We will describe decision-making organized around the shared interests which members of any given economic enterprise are presumed to have. To quote Horvat, "The Yugoslav economic system consists of autonomous, self-governing, work organizations and individual producers in market and non-market sectors and of government machinery. The task of the latter is to use *non-administrative* means in coordinating the activities of market and non-market agents and to organize public administration in certain fields of common interest (judiciary, defense, foreign affairs, etc.)." [15] Yugoslavia has arrived at this system through continuous experimentation in which economic problems have been solved for the most part, not by

[14] See, for example, Milton Kotler, *Neighborhood Government: The Local Foundations of Political Life* (Indianapolis, Ind.: Bobbs-Merrill, 1969).

[15] Branko Horvat, "Yugoslav Economic Policy in the Post-War Period: Problems, Ideas, Institutional Developments," supplement to the *American Economic Review*, 61 (1971), p. 95.

the manipulation of instruments within a given framework, but by what Horvat calls "an endless series of reorganizations" of the economic system.

In describing the present system, it is useful to distinguish *decentralization* from *self-government*. The system which has evolved in Yugoslavia has reached its present form after passing through stages of centralized directive planning, followed by various reforms which provided for increasing degrees of decentralization, culminating in the present self-management. After the reform of 1961 considerable decentralization took place, but a certain amount of the economic initiative and responsibility was decentralized to communal (local) government units. The reforms of 1965 and subsequent years have gone much further in shifting the burden of economic management to the working organizations themselves. The term "working organization" was given constitutional status in 1963, and includes enterprises and other business establishments, but also includes medical, educational, and cultural institutions which typically operate outside normal market mechanisms in Western countries. Indeed, the visitor to Yugoslavia is often surprised to find such social organizations working on a self-supporting market basis which goes much further toward competition than is found in capitalist countries. For the purposes of this book it is sufficient to note that the Yugoslavs have passed through some of the experiences typical of political-administrative decentralization en route to their present form of organization.

The Yugoslav political economy is still in the course of development. The reforms, or institutional changes, began in 1958, and in 1971 further modification of the constitution was approved. But throughout this period there has as yet been no step toward recentralization. The record to date is one of steady erosion of what the Yugoslavs recognize as the state, and of its servant, bureaucracy. In dramatic contrast to the early postwar period of central planning, the state power cannot constitutionally interfere with the autonomy of individual enterprises, nor interfere in the governance of those enterprises by the workers. This decentralization of economic life has caused a decentralization of social and political life, as well, sometimes threatening the very conception of the national state.

Several principles of the control of economic and social activity are relevant to the American scene. First, direct workers' control does not mean that every worker is a manager. Rather, the workers elect a council which, in turn, elects a managing board and a director. While this arrangement appears similar to the election of Model Cities boards by residents of model neighborhoods in the United States, there are some very significant differences. In the worker enterprises voting members have important direct stakes in management practices, and only those actually working in the enterprise vote. And it is also different from stock ownership in that nonworkers are excluded from participation and all votes are in principle equal. The enterprise, in turn, is expected to make its way in competitive markets.

Second, these market principles are relaxed only slightly for schools, planning offices, government service bureaus, hospitals, and other enterprises supplying public or merit goods. This relaxation takes the form of indirect subsidies to the supplier so that costs can be kept within the reach of all potential users, or at least at the level of socially desired usage. To avoid creating supplier bureaucracies, the system interposes a consumer interest in the form of self-governing "interest unions." These unions receive funds from parliament and in turn buy the services of the public producers on behalf of consumers. There is thus some degree of competition in the public sector— the supplier units are independent and self-governing—and self-serving in the government bureaucracy is reduced. In practice, however, ordinary market enterprises are under some political pressure to buy certain of these services, or to contribute to special funds which will buy the services. This pressure arises in part from the socialist commitment to a degree of egalitarianism and from the desire to provide some services in accord with need.

Finally, federal, republican, and local authorities are not abolished. A degree of state apparatus remains. The federal government retains control of foreign policy, the army, the national bank, taxation, some direct investment in enterprises such as railways and ports, and some redistributive functions, such as the Fund for the Developing Areas. But it is notable that the state does not directly provide social services, such as health, education, welfare, or housing, in the manner of our overlapping, layer-cake federal system. Thus many of the decentralization issues in the United States do not emerge in Yugoslavia.

This presentation has not included an evaluation of the efficiency of the Yugoslav self-management system, or an estimation of how it works in practice, or an assessment of issues of equity. It does not adequately describe the actual practices of management such as the real autonomy of managers. A basic reason is that the dominant character of Yugoslav development is change. The ease with which Yugoslavia incorporates proposed changes into law, to the point of substantially revising the constitution, is a product of the decentralized system as well as a cause of it. These constitutional changes, moreover, understate the actual amount of continuous modification which goes on in the system, for self-governing enterprises have the right under the constitution to make laws governing their own operations. Under this most dialectical principle, enterprises can pass laws governing their own self-management that will affect the management function, distribution of income, and conduct of work. Horvat quotes Kovacevic to the effect that this produces "a continual narrowing of the area of state law and corresponding broadening of the area of so-called autonomous law." [16]

It is obviously difficult to characterize this system, which takes as its source the later works of Marx. It blends the direct action tradition of the revolutionary movements, such as the

---

[16] *Ibid.*, p. 102.

Paris communards, with native distrust of bureaucracy, and has some structural elements that would have gladdened Sorel and the anarcho-syndicalists. More useful for our purposes is to point out what is similar—and dissimilar—to American proposals for decentralization. We will also look at problems of planning that have arisen in this system.

In the course of moving from direct governmental control of the economy, the Yugoslavs gave up a certain amount of planning, devolved other planning functions to local governments and enterprises, and changed the focus of planning concerns. As early as 1952 the central planning commission relinquished direct control of economic activities and shifted to the more indirect role of influencing large, fundamental functions, such as investment, consumption, and budgets. This allowed republics, communes, and enterprises to produce their own plans more or less independently. Communes, and recently republics, have been concerned largely with physical plans—with the development of infrastructures and the associated locational concerns. Enterprises made their own economic plans, without a strict requirement to clear them with national plans.

In the course of decentralization, the Yugoslavs reduced state economic planning to monetary management and to forecasting. Instead of the centralized planning of production they spoke of decentralized planning which was conducted with consultations among enterprises about projections of supply and demand in the market, reminiscent of French "indicative planning," often without the results of the latter due to the greater independence of Yugoslav enterprises.[17] Planning was not closely coordinated throughout the layers of the federal system.[18] Thus directive planning in Yugoslavia is done principally at the republic and local (commune) levels. These plans,

[17] Stephen S. Cohen, *Modern Capitalist Planning: The French Model* (Cambridge, Mass.: Harvard University Press, 1969).

[18] Richard Burton, John Dyckman, Jack Fisher, "A Social Planning System for Yugoslavia" (paper presented at the international meeting of the Regional Science Association, Vienna, 1966).

however, do not add up to or constitute a national plan for Yugoslavia.

In this transformation the emphasis was on planning as an instrumental and not a directing force of the economy. Between the market and planning, Yugoslavia has given first place to the market as the principal expression of social preferences. In effect, the Yugoslav system has acted to encourage voluntarism as thoroughly, if somewhat differently, as Tiebout proposed to do. But it has left intercommunal and interrepublic coordination as empty as it is in the Tiebout case. Indeed, the spatial aspects of organization and planning receive little emphasis in Yugoslav plans. Unlike the Tiebout models, however, the Yugoslav system permits joint membership in more than one "club" at a time—for example, the individual is at once a member of the government of his working organization and of his local residential community, the commune. These latter are small in some regions—for example, Slovenia—so that much crossing-over of clubs takes place, with many membership combinations. The decision-making role has shifted from communal economic participation to working organizations; the latter have become the more important functional membership group.

But the communal choice is also relevant in Yugoslavia, as there are important differences in resources, in public goods, and in quality of living among the communes. Unlike the member of the hypothetical Tiebout world who enjoys perfect mobility, the real world of the Yugoslav citizen is bounded by limits of distance and availability of transportation. We might agree as a result that Yugoslavia will need still another level in its complex federal system—the metropolitan unit—if the market of spatial and work community is to facilitate the expression and satisfaction of preferences. To date, this has not been the subject of constitutional change.

Nor does the Yugoslav case display the amount of mobility needed to achieve the matching of individual preferences with local offerings. This, remarkably enough, was not the case even in the period in which communes participated directly in national economic development. In fact, the Yugoslav society is so "sticky" that interrepublican migration is not a major factor in reducing interregional income differences, despite the fact that these differences may have a greater range than the income differences within enterprises.

A paradox of the Yugoslav system is that it is both decentralized and relatively immobile spatially. Yet it does not fragment into small parts. The synergy of the system has come from its ability to deliver welfare and diffuse benefits through the economy, and from the mobilization of energy achieved by the self-management process. The system of social planning—measured by the inputs of planners or their plans—has contributed relatively little to the performance of the economy or the cohesion of the society. Nor has local (communal) government provided the cement of the system. It is true that the communes provided a transitional agency for the movement from centralized command to self-government in enterprises, largely "directing" the enterprises in the period from 1959 to 1964, but since 1968 their role in direct investment has been greatly diminished. While local ties are strong in many parts of Yugoslavia, the functions of the communes have dwindled to those of town planning, the provision of local services, and some local political processes. The planning "system" in Yugoslavia is neither really a system nor conventionally recognizable as planning.

What does exist in the form of national guidance is more characterized by negotiation than rational analysis. Centrally planned change is really accomplished by constitution-writing and revision. In this sense, the planning function at the national level is done by political people rather than technicians. As a result of a constitutional amendment in August, 1972, there will be government by a rotating "chairman of the board," who will be president on an annual basis with three representatives from each republic and two provinces. Everything will be done by negotiation. The prerogatives of the federal government are nonexistent except in the areas of defense and foreign affairs, which again must be negotiated with republican parliaments. It is anticipated that in 1973 the federal parliament will become a senate with equal representation from each of the republics. Yugoslavia will become a completely negotiated system, a confederation.

Bajt, writing in 1967, saw social decision-making moving from a *centralized autocratic directive* model to a *decentralized anarchic* model with eventual further development toward a *decentralized democratic indicative* model.[19] To achieve this last-mentioned stage, the political economy needs, as he put it, "a thoroughly elaborated and internally consistent system of economic inductors if it is to operate satisfactorily."[20] Planning practices have evolved in the direction of "inductors"—that is, economic instruments which induce enterprises into highest economic efficiency without authoritarian control—but planning, like the self-governing system, is still in evolution. The Yugoslavs have yet to demonstrate how planning can be reconciled with extreme decentralization of decision-making.

LONDON TWO-TIER GOVERNMENT

We turn now to a consideration of a third model of decentralization, the London two-tier form of government.[21] Like the Yugoslav case, the London example is a real world model; however, it is much more modest in its devolution of powers. It is much more a compromise in that it represents both a greater centralization of government at the metropolitan level and greater decentralization of power at the borough level. In this sense, it is a case of limited decentralization. However, the

---

[19] Aleksander Bajt, "Decision-Making in the Yugoslav Economy," *Economics of Planning*, 7 (1967), pp. 73–85.

[20] *Ibid.*, p. 84.

[21] For a general discussion of the history and enactment of the London two-tier form of government, see Gerald Rhodes, *The Government of London* (London: London School of Economics and Political Science, 1970).

London example has the virtue of dealing with the issue ignored in both the Tiebout and Yugoslav models, that is, the problem of coordination among autonomous governmental units.

The London two-tier form of government was created by taking the boroughs of the former City of London and combining them with the independent boroughs outside the city to form the Greater London Council. This reorganization gives greater power, both to the constituent parts of the central city, as well as to a metropolitan organization which for the first time limits the freedom of the suburbs. Each borough has equal representation on the council.

Decentralization to the borough level occurs in London only with respect to those powers already granted to local government by the central (national) government. Such powers include housing, education, sanitation, and the personal social services. However, important powers are reserved by the national government, for example, police and transportation. Such decentralization as does occur should not obscure the fact that the weight of past experience confirms the need for and tendency toward a flow of power from local to national government because local government cannot solve problems of intergovernmental equity and coordination.

The planning of housing developments by the Greater London Council is an example of the historical pattern. The experience so far does not suggest you can decentralize the important, or controversial, functions of government. At this point the outer London boroughs continue to refuse to accept inner-city residents for housing. The only solution seems to be for the national government to intervene and force the suburbs to accept these residents. However, the London example does have areas of success that are instructive for us—particularly in the social services—in decentralizing the government power concentrated in London.

The question of financing is critical in any decentralization model.[22] In the London plan, the local tax rate is set and taxes are collected by the lower-tier authority, the borough, but the upper-tier authority, the council, sets the requirement for the tax rate. National government meets over one-half the cost of the combined budget of the Greater London Council which is used to compensate for the unequal resource base among the various boroughs. The London Boroughs Association each year decides on a formula by which the contribution from the national government is distributed to the less affluent boroughs in order to fill the gap between their needs and the amount that can be raised through locally set tax rates. Londoners, from both affluent and poor boroughs, believe it is quite important to fix and raise taxes locally.

The London two-tier plan of government has had considerable appeal to those who are looking for ways to decentralize large city governments in the United States. It has been proposed, for example, as a way of dealing with the problems of New York City. The model can be most appropriately applied on the basis of specific problem areas. Waste disposal, police, and other presently overwhelming urban problems might reasonably be handled by many decentralized authorities instead of city hall.

However, the financing scheme in the London model not only seems impractical but also could be considered unconstitutional in the United States in light of the *Serrano* v. *Priest* decision.[23] The model of the New York City Board of Education seems more appropriate. A central board, with central taxing authority, sets up a central budget that equalizes allocations on

[22] For a discussion of the financing of the greater London government, see S. K. Ruck and Gerald Rhodes, *The Government of Greater London* (London: Allen and Unwin, 1970), p. 6.

[23] *Serrano* v. *Priest.* 5 Cal. 3d 584, 487 P. 2d 1241 (1971). This decision of the California Supreme Court requires the State Board of Education to adopt a school financing plan that equalizes tax expenditures among school districts. A similar ruling by the United States District Court for West Texas was overturned by the United States Supreme Court. *Rodriguez* v. *San Antonio Independent School District*, 337 F. Supp. 280 (1971).

a per capita basis to decentralized school districts. In order for decentralization to have any equalizing effect, financing must be centralized.

ADVANTAGES OF DECENTRALIZATION

We began this chapter with the observation that decentralization as a concept of public decision-making has been proffered as a solution to the dilemma between consensus and control inherent in centrally planned change. Each of the cases dealt with this issue. The Tiebout model maximized consensus by assuming a residential market in which everyone could shop around to find the community which best suited his expressed needs for public goods at a price he was willing to pay. The Yugoslav model accomplished the same objective by organizing decision-making groups around common production interests, allowing each enterprise a relatively free hand in establishing its goals and means of achieving them. The London case apparently allows for greater congruence between the provision of public goods and local preferences by organizing local government around spatially decentralized units. It should be noted that in each case increased consensus was purchased at the price of lesser control by the inclusive system needed to plan and to deal with problems of an intercommunity nature, that is, externalities and the provision of such public goods as the redistribution of income. What, then, are the advantages and disadvantages of decentralization as disclosed in these cases, and what are the implications for planning theory?

Two principal advantages emerge from the discussion of decentralization. First, decentralization as devolution of power overcomes alienation of the citizenry from their government. This has the positive effect of creating social energy in the form of encouraging and rewarding private actions on behalf of public efforts. Second, decentralization makes government responsive to the needs of more of its citizenry by breaking down delivery units to correspond with the disparate preferences of various constituencies. Decentralization seems to be justified primarily by a social-psychological benefit rather than any substantive change in the working of government. It does not lead to government doing different things, but doing the same things in a more sensitive manner.

For example, in the Yugoslav self-governing worker communes, there appears to be greater worker satisfaction, even in Detroit-type assembly-line jobs, because workers have a say in how to change that routine within the workday. They also have a voice in determining what package of goods or services the commune will purchase with the profits earned by the enterprise, for example, housing, canteens, or higher individual salaries.

However, the Yugoslavs as a nation are apparently not entirely free of the problem of alienation. Large numbers of industrial workers migrate—roughly 1,000,000 Yugoslavs are employed outside the country. This population is made up of predominantly unskilled workers, a fact which suggests that the worker communes are not only clubs, they are exclusive clubs.

The counterpart of this argument is that decentralization is a way of making government more responsive to its constituency and therefore more effective in carrying out its responsibilities. According to this view the primary problem facing large cities is the breakdown in public services resulting from a lack of congruency between the needs of the citizenry and the workings of their government. Breaking up the city into small self-governing units with respect to specific services, like sanitation and police protection, is seen as a way of tailoring such services to the peculiar life styles or needs of various constituencies.

Many advocate some sort of decentralization in urban government. The central authority has become so powerful in cities like Boston, New York, and Philadelphia that the very scope of the power prevents effective action. Increasingly public services are performed more poorly by city government, yet the cost of government persistently rises over 10 percent a year. Decentralization along the lines of the London two-tier government has been proposed as a way of improving the quality of services and giving citizens a sense of participation and belonging without drastic reallocation of power.

DISADVANTAGES OF DECENTRALIZATION

The major problem with decentralization, in the form of a devolution of power as a framework in which to undertake planned change, is that it makes difficult the achievement of equity or social justice. This problem takes several forms: (1) members of the larger system who do not belong to or do not fit into one of the decentralized units do not benefit from public goods distributed through those units; (2) decentralization provides no means of redistributing resources among unequal units; (3) a decentralized structure lacks the means for handling externalities created by individual units.

In the Yugoslav case, the benefits of the worker communes are confined to those who are members of such enterprises. For example, there is no public-housing program anywhere in Yugoslavia. Housing is provided as part of the enterprise system. If you are not a part of the enterprise system, you get no housing. In that sense, the worker commune system is a set of exclusive clubs.

Decentralization runs counter to social equality in another important respect. In the form of devolution of power, decentralization means a preserving of the status quo regarding the distribution of resources. This effect is nowhere more evident than in Yugoslavia. The very stimulus for decentralization in that country grew out of the tension which resulted from the transfer of payments from more favored republics to less favored republics. It was hoped through decentralization to circumvent this tension. In fact, however, decentralization has resulted in a reduction of transfers. Banks are using a strict rate of return rather than socialist goals of equality as the basis for making investments. The Fund for Developing Areas has thus been declining. This makes inequality "an atrocious feature of decentralization." A similar observation about the difficulties of redistribution without central intervention can be made with respect to the London two-tier system. The outer London boroughs are unwilling to share their more favorable public amenities with less favored inner London residents, and the Greater London Council which has the full power to intervene is unwilling to exercise that power. It seems that regardless of the system of government the well-to-do do not want the less well-to-do among them.

For this reason, decentralization in this country within the present municipal structure of government would be of little advantage. Metropolitan government is already balkanized with many suburban communities around the central city. Decentralization of the central city would provide no way of equalizing resources throughout the metropolitan area.

Most models of decentralization have no way of handling externalities without invoking some more inclusive decision-making system. This was recognized in the Tiebout model, and explicitly provided in the London case. In the Yugoslav system, a structure for inclusive decision-making is apparently emerging based on negotiations between republics which result in constitutional revisions. However, in the absence of successful negotiations no resolution of conflicts between coequal units is possible.

And finally, decentralization ignores the issue of those functions which can be provided only through common effort—truly public goods, such as defense and transportation. Each of the cases examined here recognized that at least some residual functions require centralized planning and administration. Few would argue that distribution of natural resources, redistribution of income, civil rights, and civil liberties are matters for local control.

IMPLICATIONS FOR CENTRALLY PLANNED CHANGE

This chapter began with the observation that centralized planning inevitably invokes a conflict between the consensus necessary to support directed change efforts, and the control necessary to execute such efforts. Decentralization as a concept of planning was examined as one alternative to resolving this conflict by organizing efforts to provide public goods on a scale which corresponds to the diverse interests of our society and thereby increases aggregate consensus.

Decentralization was examined primarily from the standpoint of a devolution of power from a centralized unit to smaller units, rather than in the form of administrative-spatial organization of bureaucratic services. Decentralization of planning and the provision of public goods inevitably takes on the characteristics of a market system and is subject to the same limitations of such systems as devices for achieving public goals.

It should be recognized that decentralization in any form works only when the self-governing units are coincident with common interest groups. In Yugoslavia, the republics are really separate nations with their own language, history, religion, and culture. In the absence of any clear-cut group identification, decentralization in the form of devolution of power will probably not result in greater effectiveness of government.

In summary, it can be said that some public functions may well be decentralized while others require greater centralization. The difficulty with the American political system is the tendency to adopt reforms indiscriminately—to operate completely in one mode rather than another. There is a need to carefully assess the differential way in which decentralization may be adopted to improve societal guidance. Each of the cases discussed in this chapter represents varying degrees of such differentiation. The Tiebout model represented the pure case of decentralization with no centralized intervention implied. The Yugoslav case represented a fluid state moving toward complete decentralization but stopping short of dissolving some central apparatus for mutual defense and foreign affairs. The London case was clearly mixed with definite functions decentralized while control of redistributive functions remained with the central government.

Assuming that the promotion of equality, protection against externalities, and the provision of public goods are of concern, some degree of centralized planning is required. However, the structure and methodology of such planning takes on some new aspects. In its simplest form, centralized planning within a decentralized framework would consist of making strategic plans centrally, sometimes referred to as *metaplanning*, and leaving fine-grain planning to be done by decentralized units. This "planning of the planning system," to borrow a term from Dror, needs elaboration.[24] The decentralization of the planning function is consistent with the recent emergence of advocacy planning methods of public decision-making. But what has been lacking in such a framework is any mechanism for aggregating the interests of competing groups. A new methodology of constitution writing is suggested. It establishes the rules whereby the member units interact, and some management of the negotiation process which resolves or coordinates inter-unit differences. And finally, some means of centralized financing is essential in order to achieve redistribution among unequal members.

[24] See his comments on the papers by Friedmann and Dyckman in the "Symposium on Changing Styles of Planning in Post Industrial America," *Public Administration Review*, 31 (May–June, 1971).

CHAPTER SIX

THE USE OF MARKET MECHANISMS IN CENTRALIZED PLANNING[1]

One response to the dilemma of consensus and control as discussed in Chapter 5 is the decentralizing of structures for planned change, or the devolution of power. We turn here to an alternative proposal—the provision of public goods and services through the private marketplace. A number of questions arise. What are market mechanisms? Can they be used for public purposes? Does reliance on the market relieve the necessity for centralized planning? What are the conditions under which the marketplace could function in these areas? And what are the limitations of the marketplace for achieving public purposes?

Much of the action pursuant to centrally planned change involves the production and distribution of public goods by governmental agencies. We are already familiar with such goods and services as health care, welfare services, housing, and education. Recent federal programs such as the War on Poverty, the Model Cities program, and Manpower Development and Training also reflect the method of governmental planning for social services *and* government provision of the services through federal agencies. Politicians express social priorities, and public bureaucracies act on these social needs through the administration of particular programs. It is at the point when a social ob-

[1] This chapter is based in part on a paper entitled "Clients, Consumers and Citizens," prepared by Anthony H. Pascal, the Rand Corporation.

jective necessitates new or expanded production and distribution of some good or, more commonly, some service, that market mechanisms can come into play. The use of vouchers places the production and distribution of such services within the marketplace rather than in the usual setting of centralized bureaucracy as both provider and distributor. The use of the open market is not the goal; rather, market mechanisms are seen as tools to achieve social goals.

THE NATURE OF PUBLIC GOODS AND SERVICES

In traditional economic theory, public goods and services are taken to be those commodities that meet either of two conditions: (1) The exclusion of some relevant group from the enjoyment of the good or service is not possible. Thus the full benefits of production cannot be appropriated by the producer through sales. National defense and generalized police protection are notable examples. (2) Consumption of the commodity is not subject to crowding, that is, utilization by one person does not reduce consumption opportunities for others.[2] Here the classic example is information, which, of course, does not get used up as it is consumed. Both cases provide grounds for public responsibility to make the goods available either by governmental production and distribution or by subsidies to expand private production and distribution. On their own, private firms would always choose to produce too little of such goods because they could not capture the full benefits of production through sales or because they would restrict consumers to those willing to pay a price even though the admission of additional consumers would lower no one's consumption opportunities.

There is a third type of production in which governments often engage that does not meet either of the criteria for pure public goods—natural monopolies or situations in which, be-

[2] Armen Alchian, William Allen, *University Economics* (3rd ed.; Belmont, Calif.: Wadsworth, 1964), pp. 147–154.

cause of technical considerations, a good is most cheaply provided by a single producer. The government has the option of regulating a private supplier or producing the good itself. Without regulation the private monopolist will find it to his advantage to produce less than needed and to artificially inflate the price. Utilities and some sorts of transport are the common examples, and governments often choose public production because they rightly perceive the political difficulties of truly effective regulation of private producers.

One final type of service for which government is the only logical producer is the protection of persons unable to provide for their own basic human needs. Medical care to orphans, counseling to juveniles, treatment for the insane, or services to addicts or alcoholics are examples. In this area of public goods, utilization of voucher/market mechanisms is clearly inappropriate, since the basic necessary presupposition—competence on the part of the user of the service—is not valid.

It should be noted that equality can be considered a public good. The reliance on voluntary gifts or transfers between people to achieve equality will be insufficient, since any one person's effort is not necessary to receive the benefit; he can depend upon his neighbor's giving. Thus, a role for government arises in such activities. However, the activities undertaken to bring about equality may not be public goods. Thus housing per se is not a public good, but subsidization of housing costs for low income families is. Of course, many programs that extend equality take the form of transfers of money from richer to poorer. In these cases, the public good—satisfaction generated by living in a more equal society—is produced as a result of the cash transfer; there is no other production, and the public purse is the logical transfer channel. But programs that seek to extend equality by making transfers of goods—through housing, medical, or educational services—can utilize the voucher/market approach.

This digression into the philosophy of political economics demonstrates that recognition on the part of government that a commodity must be made more widely and equally available does not require that government is the best producer of that same commodity. For the greater part of what we traditionally refer to as public services, there are other appropriate means of production and distribution. For such services as education, skill training, day care, recreation, health care, housing, retirement insurance, and many others, the voucher/market mechanism is at least a viable, and perhaps a superior, alternative.

VOUCHER/MARKET SYSTEMS

In a voucher/market system, some group or groups in society are identified and granted the right to utilize a given service. The tangible expression of that right takes the form of a voucher issued by the government. The holder of a voucher is expected to find his own supplier in a marketplace of potential suppliers.[3] The supplier in turn will be compensated for the service he renders, either by payment of a bill he submits to the appropriate government agency or directly by the voucher holder, who is then usually required to show the agency that he has in fact utilized the service. The quality of the service may be enhanced by stipulation of the payer agency, and in some cases only suppliers meeting certain conditions may be permitted to receive compensation. For example, educational payments may require coverage of certain subject matter, or medical payments may be reserved for personnel with certain qualifications. Suppliers could range from existing governmental institutions, to not-for-profit private organizations, such as neighborhood groups, churches, or cooperatives, to profit-seeking private firms.

Voucher/market systems are neither very new nor very rare. Many college scholarships have voucher features, though they have historically been provided by philanthropic institutions; the National Merit Scholarships reflect increased government

[3] For a classical discussion of the voucher/market system, see Milton Friedman, *Capitalism and Freedom* (Chicago, Ill.: University of Chicago Press, 1962).

use of this technique. An early and very large government voucher program, of course, was the GI bill's education and training benefits following World War II. Veterans were granted the right to a college education or to vocational training; the government provided financing, while the veteran shopped for an institution that could provide the courses that interested him. Food stamps are the equivalent of vouchers and so are the identification cards which certify that the holder is eligible for Medicare benefits.

The rent supplement program of the 1965 Housing and Urban Development Act, on the other hand, does not qualify as a voucher system. In that program, the contract is between the government financing agency and the supplier of the service, here the builder/owner. The consumer's ability to enter the market is not affected in this hybrid form of housing with private owners but publicly financed. Similar government-supplier contracting arrangements are common in day-care and recreation services.

Advantages and Disadvantages of Vouchers

Vouchers do promise some very real benefits. Most of them stem from the effects of competition among suppliers of the service. Increased efficiency comes immediately to mind. Those suppliers whose costs of operation exceed those of their rivals are forced out of the market. (Of course, unlike private goods, public goods have inherent quality standards and this advantage of competitively effected efficiency depends on the assumption that the vouchers will cover typical costs at a certain level of quality.) It is difficult to think of government producers of goods or services that have gone out of business because their costs were too high. Innovation is also encouraged by approval of users who hold the powerful vouchers. The spread of successful innovation would be hastened by the force of competition. None of these effects characterize the production of public services by governmental agencies which tend, instead, to have monopolistic power over their "markets." Think of the neighborhood public school or the local public clinic in the days before Medicaid.

The other side of the coin of competition is freeedom of choice. Services that are justified by their public good aspect tend to be universal in their provision (for example, schooling). However, in some cases, they are provided on a selected basis to people who are poor or otherwise disadvantaged (for example, publicly financed housing). We have been bound, for the latter case, by a pervasive but largely unexamined assumption that such people are not to be trusted to make the kind of choices that the nonpoor make continually. By extending freedom of choice, the voucher system may have important side benefits of encouraging individual responsibility and restoring personal pride.

A third advantage of voucher schemes stems from the fact that the subsidized and the unsubsidized consumers will tend to mix in the market, a feature that governmentally produced services often lack. Despite pious political rhetoric, public housing is still built in poor neighborhoods, and unlike trade and professional schools, public vocational programs draw almost entirely from the hard-core unemployed group. Granting the disadvantaged the power to choose suppliers of the services they require may reduce the stigma that now attaches to the consumption of these services in public institutions and may thereby foster integration in the society. The Medicaid experience, however, suggests that achieving integration with the voucher system may not be so easy. Under Medicaid, voucher clients were often shunned by private practitioners because of the red tape involved in securing payment and because of the loss of freedom in accounting for income with respect to taxation. Given this experience we cannot be certain that voucher holders will not end up receiving second-class services instead of becoming integrated with the social strata in the open market.

On the other hand, the voucher system provides the opportunity for "positive segregation," the formation of consumer groups in the market around some common interest which cannot be satisfied on an individual basis. Those who prefer to maintain some group identity apart from the majority—for example, black nationalists—have the option of doing so under the voucher system. They need only to find enough like-minded voucher holders to found their own schools or housing developments. The use of vouchers also enables the formation of consumer groups (for instance, cooperatives) that may be able to create the means of production of a new product or command sufficient interest within the market for an industry to create a new product or service.

And last, the use of vouchers to provide public goods and services enables the government to be more critical in evaluating public expenditures and in pursuing the interests of consumers. Since the government is not the producer, it is free of bureaucratic self-interest disguised as public interest in evaluating services rendered. The government itself does not need to prove the success of a specific program in terms of benefits received. Much more care is likely to be exercised in scrutinizing what is being purchased with tax dollars. The use of vouchers also avoids an important misuse of the technique of awarding government contracts for provision of a particular public good or service. For example, vouchers would eliminate the collusion that often occurs between big developers and bureaucratic officials in contractual arrangements for providing subsidized housing. Since the voucher mechanism distributes this public assistance on a more atomistic and widespread basis, it makes corruption more difficult and forces the developer to make his profit in an open competitive situation.

The voucher/market approach has not escaped attack. Some of the criticisms are entirely valid and point to the limitations of the method, others are troublesome but can be overcome. However, some criticisms tend to be quite specious and can be dismissed. Among the specious attacks is the charge that needless duplication of facilities will result. The technical characteristics of the production process and the variation in taste among potential buyers will determine whether more than one supplier is superfluous and wasteful. For most personal services—the most comparable industry in the private sector on which cost studies are available—the optimal size of establishment tends to be quite small.[4] There are lots of beauty salons because customers want convenient locations and have varying preferences for style and atmosphere. There are very few public high schools, not because of economy or quality, but because the providers have little incentive to be either convenient or responsive to individual preferences. And it is not uncommon to find the political system producing a plethora of nearly identical suppliers. A visit to any city's poverty area will quickly demonstrate a number of duplicated job training and counseling programs.

Nor does opening up the supply base of public goods and services mean closing down existing governmental services. For example, public schools are not necessarily abandoned under the voucher system. Those public providers which remain competitive in the market are just as likely to profit as private providers. There are many public school systems that are good enough to survive as systems or individual schools. Thus the institution of the voucher mechanism does not necessarily mean that past and current public investments in existing services will be wasted.

Another line of criticism holds that competition is likely to reduce quality. The rationale appears to be that cost-cutting pressures will result in less than adequate standards of public services. The validity of the criticism suggests two necessary corollaries to the voucher system. First, the financing provided by the vouchers must be sufficiently generous so that the average supplier can meet the quality standard. Second, it is

---

[4] Joseph P. Newhouse, "The Economics of Group Practice," *Journal of Human Resources*, 8 (Winter, 1973), pp. 37–56; David Schwartzman, "The Growth of Sales Per Man Hour in Retail Trade" in *Production and Productivity in the Service Industry*, ed. V. R. Fuchs (New York: Columbia University Press for the National Bureau of Economics Research, 1969), pp. 201–229.

undeniably important to establish official quality standards, the violation of which will void the suppliers' right to cash the voucher. However, it should be recognized that many public agencies under the present monopolistic conditions have themselves been rightly accused of providing low-quality service. Thus the present pattern of public provision is no guarantee of high quality service.

A more fundamental objection to the voucher approach, one already touched upon, questions the basic competency of consumers to make rational choices among competing suppliers. Often such doubts are expressed only about people who use public services, a bias against the ability of poor people to decide for themselves. But increasingly one branch of contemporary social criticism questions the ability of any individual consumer to choose wisely. This argument in its most radical form is based on the assertion that there is no such thing as consumer sovereignty, or the ability of consumers to influence producers. The production of goods in a capitalist economy is controlled by persons who are alleged to be unresponsive to consumer interests. Although the planning of production is decentralized throughout a corporate structure, it is nevertheless performed by persons of wealth who control the means of production. Producers are free to determine what choices will be offered the consumer.

Control over the decision of what should be produced, so runs this argument, should be in the hands of consumers and not the wealthy few. To leave the decision in the hands of private producers limits the ability of society to establish social priorities, to raise basic questions about what products or services are to be produced, or where investments should go, for example, into more housing or more highly styled clothing. The only way to distribute goods and services to satisfy consumer needs is for consumers to have control over the production and supply side of the market through direct public ownership.

The "incompetency of the consumer" is argued most vociferously in discussions of the power of advertising. People are alleged to have too little of the right sort of information—about the technical characteristics of the product, its long-term consequences, its social effects—and are overloaded with the wrong sort which they are fed primarily by the advertising industry. Through the power of advertising, producers can determine what consumers want to buy—they can generate a demand for their product. While we recognize the enormous impact of advertising and its role in society, experience shows that it is not necessarily misleading or fraudulent. Advertising is itself neutral. It can encourage cigarette smoking but also advocate "kicking the habit." It is used to promote family planning and residential integration as well as underarm deodorants and exclusive suburbs. There seems no compelling reason why advertising by organizations hoping to lure voucher holders could not be stringently regulated, as is now established in the cigarette and liquor market.

In a later section, a number of ways in which "good" advertising (that is, providing useful information) might be arranged will be discussed. We have no evidence to support the pessimistic prediction that users of public services will succumb to the lures of fraudulent promotion but be blind to prudent and responsible guidance.

Observers have pointed out that the adoption a few years ago of a voucher scheme for health care—the Medicare and Medicaid programs—resulted in an enormous escalation in the costs of medical services not only for the government, which foots the bill for Medicare beneficiaries, but for nonbeneficiaries as well, who are feeling a ripple effect in their own escalating medical bills.[5] The facts are accurate but are an unjust criticism of the voucher system in general. The Medicare program was designed and put into effect with almost no provisions for the obvious effect of increased demand on medical services. In spite of what they knew, Medicare planners did little to increase

[5] Edward R. Fried, *et al.*, *Setting National Priorities: The 1974 Budget* (Washington, D.C.: The Brookings Institution, 1973), pp. 128–129.

supply. Significantly increasing the number of places available in medical schools, rationalizing state-licensing provisions for practitioners, encouraging the use of auxiliary personnel, and providing for more training for such people would all have been important steps in helping the supply respond to the increase in demand generated by Medicare. Whatever was done along these lines was belated and piecemeal. The fault lay not in the voucher concept but in the cowardice or myopia which prevented any meaningful confrontation with the professional oligopoly which supplies American medical services. That other applications of the voucher approach will benefit from this sad experience is to be hoped, if not anticipated. But we cannot ignore another, more important, result of Medicare: the poor and the elderly do receive better medical treatment than they did when their only recourse was public clinics. And they are not likely to disdain the freedom of choice and the absence of stigma which now characterize their experience with health care.

We turn now to a number of criticisms of the voucher/market system which indicate its limitations in meeting public objectives. Principal among these is the achievement of a socially desirable income distribution. Alterations in the distribution of income among a given population are not a function of the market; the distribution must be fixed by extra-market mechanisms. Since the most important source of consumer disadvantage under present conditions among poor people is inadequate income, the question naturally arises, why not redistribute income or give direct cash transfers instead of setting up a complicated apparatus for dispensing vouchers? The answer lies in the fact that giving lump sums of unencumbered cash would not achieve important social goals. There is a public interest in encouraging people to consume more of certain things than others. It is better for a family to purchase milk and corn meal than cigarettes and beer. Adequate housing is more desirable than purchase of a private means of transportation. If these individual choices are in fact ones that society should encourage,

146 Centrally Planned Change

then the two alternatives are vouchers or the public production of goods and services which are then given to particular consumers.

The voucher/market system does not assure socially desirable levels of consumption in all cases. When price elasticity of demand for the service or good is very nearly zero—that is, when the demand for a given good or service is nearly constant—the voucher has the same effect on the consumer's behavior as the direct income transfer. Since a voucher system is likely to be more costly to administer, it would have no advantage. The second case in which vouchers are likely to have much the same effect as income transfers is when the vouchers can be rather easily cashed or transferred from a check for a specific good or service into money. The food stamp program is subject to both of these conditions. The price elasticity of demand for food at the margin is very close to zero, even for poor people. And, in addition, many people have figured out ways to cash in food stamps for money. At best all you can say is that if you give a voucher, about sixty cents out of a dollar will be spent as the donor intended. If you give cash, the amount which will be spent on any given good or service will depend on the income elasticity for that good or service.

A third condition under which direct income transfer or redistribution would be preferable to the use of vouchers is when the voucher/market system is extended across all sectors of consumption, thus restricting choice much more than in selective public provision of goods and services. If we define how much money people ought to spend, not just on housing but also for food, health care, day care, and so forth, the resultant composite voucher system would determine both the items in the minimum marketbasket and how much people ought to spend on each item. Very few trade-offs would be possible. If the goal is consumer sovereignty, income guarantees are more appropriate than the voucher system. But if the goal is to change consumption patterns, the voucher system is the more appropriate approach. Unless income guarantees are very large—which at this time seems very unlikely—the changes in consumption level of the eligible persons would be negligible. *Income equalization would enable the poor to have greater equity in satisfying their expressed interests. Vouchers would provide greater freedom of choice for people of all income levels to satisfy socially desired consumption.*

Does the distribution of income in the country make any difference in deciding how feasible it is to use the voucher/market system? At most what you can expect from the market is that if a sufficient demand for a good is expressed, that good will be made available. Items for which a consumer cannot find enough like-minded potential buyers will not be produced. If the scale is large enough, the market will find ways of providing all sorts of products. To that extent, the feasiblity of the voucher system is a function of the income distribution. If you change the income distribution, there will be markets for things which may not now exist just because of scale.

The voucher system can be modified to achieve some degree of income redistribution. For example, the size of the voucher could be income-dependent so that bigger vouchers go to poor families. They could also be reserved exclusively for poor families, such as is the case with food stamps. The point is that a voucher system does not necessarily further a policy of income redistribution.

A second type of social objective which cannot be achieved through market mechanisms has to do with structural changes in intergroup relations, such as racial integration. Indeed, the voucher/market system could hamper the achievement of such objectives. The use of vouchers for public education, for example, could result in the greater segregation of individual schools in a period when public policy is trying to achieve greater desegregation. It may be necessary for inner-city parents to pay part of their vouchers for a busing service, or for the government to provide that service. Incentives may have to be provided to entrepreneurs to achieve a certain racial balance in their school enrollment.

With respect to equal educational opportunity, additional

problems arise. The private entrepreneur is going to respond to the most profitable opportunities for setting up his educational establishment. How do you bribe the entrepreneur to set up his private schools in the ghettos, at a price which can be covered by the voucher and at a level of quality which he may be providing in the suburb? What if no private supplier will come into an area of demand? A differential voucher system would have to be worked out. If it is more expensive, if there are more risks, if it takes higher salaries to attract good teachers into a ghetto, the value of the vouchers for people in that area would be raised. If the vouchers had to be so large that it would be inequitable to give them to well-off children, some method of discounting the voucher in the income tax return can be used so that people pay back on the voucher in direct proportion to their income.

Yet the voucher/market system may inadvertently lead to structural change by undoing existing structural arrangements through the cumulative effect of individual decisions. Racial discrimination in the field of housing provides an example. Evidence in some instances suggests that when ability to pay is not a problem prejudicial impediments to open housing might be more successfully overcome through the market mechanisms than through direct government provision. There are a certain number of upper-middle–class black families in almost every upper-middle–class neighborhood in the country. There are almost no public housing projects in such neighborhoods. In the absence of an explicit public policy fostering structural change, such as in *Shannon* v. *H.U.D.* regarding the location of public housing in racially segregated neighborhoods, the voucher/market system may do more to create such change.[6] It enables individual actions which in the aggregate may result in more desegregation than is possible through the public provision of goods and services which by necessity must conform to public policy and established mores.

[6] *Shannon* v. *U.S. Department of Housing and Urban Development*, 436 F. 2d 809 (1970).

But until barriers to an open market are broken down, the market itself is not free and the voucher cannot be depended upon to have its full desired effect. A dual market based on group characteristics, such as race, ethnicity, and social class, must be abolished if vouchers are really to create freedom of choice.

In some areas of the city, namely the central core, the market has broken down completely and has ceased to function, for example, in Baltimore, as Stegman has concluded, as has Sternlieb in Newark, and Lowrey in New York City.[7] In such areas there are people with houses who do not want them, and there are people without houses who do want them, but there is no mechanism to effect any transfer. The institutions of the market that the larger society relies upon for the sale, maintenance, and operation of housing simply do not exist in the inner city for a number of reasons. There are few sellers because of higher costs of operating housing in the inner city due to vandalism, more rapid tenant turnover, higher interest rates, a discriminatory tax policy, and so forth. The city of Baltimore, for example, would not buy inner-city houses at the value the city had assessed them. Yet landlords must pay taxes on these assessed values. Low income per se has been found not to be the major cause of substandard occupancy in the inner city of Baltimore. A number of people are paying at a rate high enough to command a good deal of housing that exists in the metropolitan areas. But access to that housing is blocked. Housing vouchers would not accomplish very much unless new institutions are created or at least until those kinds of problems are dealt with.

In summary, it can be said that the voucher/market system may be useful in achieving public objectives when those objectives have to do with the provision of individualized goods or

[7] Michael A. Stegman, *Housing Investment in the Inner City: The Dynamics of Decline* (Cambridge, Mass.: MIT Press, 1972); George Sternlieb, *The Tenement Landlord* (New Brunswick, N.J.: Rutgers University Press, 1966); and Ira S. Lowrey, Joseph S. De-Salvo, Barbara M. Woodfill, *Rental Housing in New York City, Volume II, The Demand for Shelter* (New York: New York City Rand Institute, 1971).

services. But the voucher system cannot be expected to achieve public objectives which are structural in character—the distribution of income, improvement in intergroup relations, or the openness of the market itself.

Some perspective on these issues can be gained from European countries which have had more experience than the United States with the voucher/market system. Many forms of tax relief attached to the provision of particular services are very much the same in principle. Australia relies primarily on tax relief for pensions, medical care, education, and housing, all of which are a form of voucher. In England there are improvement grants for housing, as well as family allowances for children as long as they are attending school. When they drop out of school, the family is no longer entitled to the allowance, making it in fact an educational voucher. In both these cases the program touches almost exclusively the middle class. Vouchers tend to go to people who already have money to spend. They tend to be ineffective in changing the structure of supply and demand. They perpetuate expenditure patterns that people are already accustomed to, and they encourage suppliers that already exist to meet existing kinds of demand. For this reason foreign observers are less sanguine about their benefits than American proponents of the system.

Ways of Improving the Voucher/Market System

The review of advantages and disadvantages of the voucher/market approach should help illuminate some of the companion programs necessary to make it a success. Consumer education comes first to mind. This may take the form of positive advertising, as noted earlier, by a governmental consumer agency. Some of it would result from competitive suppliers advertising their own services.

In many cases, provision of information to consumers will not prove sufficient and the public agency will find it necessary to certify or even to license suppliers. The risk in doing so, however, must be recognized. Producers in a given industry have a way of gaining control over regulatory mechanisms, as evidenced in the health field and in the transportation and communications industries, thereby impeding the free market system.[8]

The Medicare case should point out the importance of attention to the supply side in fields where voucher systems are to be employed. Artificial barriers to entry can be particularly pernicious. Suppose vouchers were to be applied on a significant scale to day care services. Suppose also that day care professionals and agencies, public and private, had the power to exclude new personnel and new institutions by means of state licensing boards. Who would doubt that the cost of day care to the government and to those parents who were not eligible to receive vouchers would skyrocket?

The establishment of powerful ombudsman agencies would also contribute much to the equitable and efficient operation of voucher schemes. Systematic procedures for investigating complaints by consumers who use government-supplied vouchers and provisions for prevention and correction of wrongs through sanctions of various kinds seem a useful and legitimate adjunct. It is quite possible that the ombudsman would chastise poor performance or shoddy practices with a bit more vigor when the culprit was an outside institution and not a group of civil service colleagues. It may be worthwhile to extend the voucher principle to allow people to spend some of their voucher money in buying technical advice and advocacy services.

In any event, it must be recognized that the voucher/market system alone is an insufficient instrument for achieving social policy objectives. It is not a substitute for income redistribution nor is it a means of achieving that objective. There must be some form of market regulation or public effort to eliminate oligopolies to assure the freedom of choice desired and to protect the consumer against excessive prices. In the absence of ad-

[8] John Kenneth Galbraith, *The New Industrial State* (2nd ed., rev.; Boston: Houghton-Mifflin, 1971).

equate knowledge and information on the part of consumers some provision for consumer education is required in order to make the demand side of the market effective. And finally, certain compensatory mechanisms or incentives will have to accompany the use of vouchers in order to achieve social objectives which cannot result from entrepreneurial initiatives.

OTHER USES OF THE MARKET

The use of vouchers is but one of several ways in which the market could be used by a central government to achieve public policy objectives. While space does not allow their elaboration, a brief recognition of these alternatives will indicate possible areas of further exploration.

1. One alternative is the use of contracts of various types, including performance contracts, between the government and the private sector, including nonprofit organizations. Although recent experimentation with contracts in the field of education have not shown improved results over public provision of education, their failure to do less poorly in a short period of time can be considered as evidence that the contract procedure is at least viable.[9] Contracts have been more suc-

---

[9] A careful dissection of the experiment in Gary suggests a rather more complex story than what has generally been reported. It appears that the profit function to these contractors was very poorly specified. The profit function, in effect, was the following: the contractor would get $800 for every child who, at the end of a certain period, passed over the national median in reading and math tests. As a result the contractor divided the class into three groups. The group for which $800 would not be sufficient to pass the national median, he ignored; in the group for which $800 might make a difference in whether or not they passed the national median he concentrated essentially all of his resources and techniques; and a third group who were going to pass over the national median regardless of what the contractor did, he also ignored. It appears that there was not much difference in the average performance of the class as a whole relative to the control group. But the group of middle-range students for which it paid the contractor to concentrate his attention did phenomenally better than the control group. The other groups actually fell absolutely in terms of their performance. Furthermore, the parents and the children in these groups perceived what was going on and showed a

cessfully used in the space field. Whatever its value, the moon program proved to be one of the most phenomenally successful public programs of the 1960s, and NASA made greater use of private contracting for components than almost any other government agency. The Atomic Energy Commission, in spite of its having the most sensitive security problems of any governmental organization, has been successful in contracting out security services.

2. Another approach to achieving public objectives is to make the market itself work rather than to substitute government programs for the present inadequacies of the market. In the health field, government activity could be withdrawn rather than extended as a means of breaking up medical cartels. For example, proprietary medical schools and health facilities would be encouraged in contrast to governmental or nonprofit facilities which are controlled by professional providers of service.

3. Another example of the use of the market for public purposes is private government, such as new towns like Reston and Columbia, retirement communities, and shopping centers. These private governments have the character of internalizing some externalities of mutual association of different peoples and of different types of commercial activities. These people provide substitutes for public services at their own cost but are subject to the same taxes as people who do not, so they pay a double bill. Only if their private activities are extraordinarily productive will it be worthwhile for them to stay in operation.

4. In the area of social insurance, the auto-liability model of bonding and insurance could be extended to pro-

disproportionate dropout rate from that experiment. So the Gary experiment should be judged as having produced just what would be expected given the specifications of the contract.

grams to protect against the financial risks of retirement and illness. The auto-liability model is based on the assumption that an individual while engaged in a specific activity, such as driving a car, may commit an act injurious to someone else. Since there is always the possibility that the offender may be unable to compensate the injured party, he is required by law to demonstrate his capacity to assume such a liability through insurance coverage or posting a bond prior to being permitted to engage in the activity. If the objective of the social insurances is to protect the public against having to pick up the dependency costs of people who cannot adequately provide for themselves, then the auto-liability model would be an alternative to governmental provision of insurance. For example, people would either post a bond, or prove that they have acquired an annuity or medical insurance of a certain value. They can shop for insurance anywhere they want. This approach would do two things. It would permit people to shop for the annuity of their choice rather than being subject to the specific one offered by the government. It would also channel monies now being used to finance public outlays for such insurance into financing additions to the capital base of the country.

5. Another government action involving greater use of the private market is a change in the tax structure to make it easier for private people or the government to assemble land parcels without the use of eminent domain. One device would be a self-assessed property tax in which people place a value on their property at which they would be prepared to sell. The tax, then, is based on their estimate of that value. Property in this case would be continuously on the market at the value set by the owner himself.

6. The market could be used to control overuse of specific services. Traffic congestion might be attacked by con-

verting public highways into private highways and placing congestion charges on their use. The problem at present is that the public sector maintains a continuous interest in underpricing activities because it uses the revealed evidence of excess demand, in this case traffic congestion, as the basis for greater direct appropriation to provide more of the activity. One way to institutionalize congestion charges would be to create corporations for facilities that tend to become congested. These corporations would be free to charge rates that are realistic to the demand.

While these suggestions are provocative, they must be viewed critically from the standpoint of social policy. In any of these proposals the question of equity, or the relative ability of people in different social strata to pay their way in the market, is completely ignored. For example, the auto-liability principle for provision of social insurance fails to recognize that the poor are likely to buy the least adequate policy available because of their inability to pay for more.

IMPLICATIONS FOR CENTRALIZED PLANNING

This discussion demonstrates a variety of ways in which the private sector or market mechanisms could be used to achieve public or social objectives without resorting to direct provision by government. However, from this discussion, it should be clear that market mechanisms are an adjunct to but do not eliminate the necessity for centralized governmental intervention.

The use of market mechanisms simply changes the nature of centralized planning and indeed frees government to play a more critical role in evaluating public expenditures in terms of consumer interests. When removed from the role of direct provider, the government is free to play a more vital role as planner and advocate of public interests. Such a planning style would have the following characteristics.

1. *Specifying public objectives.* In any use of market mechanisms, a centralized decision is required to delineate the objectives to be served by such market forces and to determine the criteria for judging when those purposes are achieved. For example, before a voucher/market system is to be used, a number of centralized decisions must be made about the services to be covered, the size of the voucher, who should receive it, and the criteria for measuring the effectiveness of its use.

2. *Regulation of the market.* If market mechanisms are to be used, both suppliers and consumers must be guaranteed free access to that market. As in the case of housing, any discrimination which restricts the access of some consumers to the market must be eliminated. As in the case of medical care, any restrictions on the access of suppliers to the market, such as the recruitment, training, and licensing of medical personnel, must be eliminated, or else prices must be controlled. These activities suggest not only reforming the market before certain programs are launched but also continuous surveillance and regulation of the market as the programs operate.

3. *Supplementation of market mechanisms.* In instituting certain public programs through the market, it may be desirable to supplement market operations in order to achieve the public objectives more adequately. This may take the form of weighting entitlements to benefits to provide some equalization, or it may involve providing incentives to suppliers to undertake production of goods which are not profitable, or to underwrite risks. Supplementation may involve performance contracting or incentives tied to a specific type of demand in the market.

4. *Public provision of certain goods.* The government will have to directly provide certain goods and services because the market cannot. Examples of such goods and services are busing to achieve school desegregation, the

redistribution of income as a public good, services which are natural monopolies, and services to those individuals in the society who are incapable of participating in the open market.

5. *Evaluation.* Last, even without supplementation or the direct provision of public goods, reliance on market mechanisms requires a centralized activity of evaluation. In fact, the evaluative function of government may be enhanced through this approach.

CHAPTER SEVEN

THE TECHNOLOGY
OF PLANNING[1]

The previous chapters have explored two possible strategies to resolve the apparent dilemma between consensus and control in centralized planning. However, in both decentralization of decision-making and the use of market mechanisms, technology becomes a critical factor in their successful realization. Technologies are required no matter what instrumentalities are introduced.

Two major areas require exploration. The first question is the extent to which analytical tools, usually associated with the concept of central planning, are useful in the decentralized context. Systems analysis, benefit-cost analysis, cost-effectiveness studies, and forecasting all are usually posited on the model of a strong central authority. The second is the feasibility and potential impact of techniques not usually associated with central planning, such as fiscal policies, monetary controls, and regulatory controls (for example, the use of zoning in land-use planning).

PURPOSE OF TECHNOLOGY

Planning technology, as discussed in the literature, implies attempts to bring rational perspectives and supporting methodologies to problem-solving activities and decision-making. How-

[1] This chapter is based in part on a paper, "Up from Failure," prepared by Allen Schick, the Brookings Institution.

ever, widespread agreement on the operational level has not followed the general acceptance of this concept. The conflict is not with the idea of more rational planning but rather with the application of specific methodologies. One point of view proposes that planning can and should be equated with rational decision-making. Decisions should be based on technical analysis, and the analysis, if it is comprehensive, will inevitably resolve conflicts and identify appropriate choices. Critics of the rational model see the problems that planners face as caused by inadequate analyses resulting in high levels of uncertainty, and invariably this leads to less than rational courses of action. The final selection of a strategy or course of action is relegated to a political process. Whereas planning technology is viewed as objective input leading to more comprehensive approaches to problem solution, political decision-making based on negotiation and bargaining among competing interest groups invariably leads to compromise, rather than concrete, rational strategies.

The counterargument places planning within the political process where, so the argument goes, it should remain. In a pluralistic society such as ours decision-makers are confronted with a large number of social needs, each important in its own right, but with resources inadequate for dealing with the entire set. Proponents of this view feel rational decision-making should be encouraged but shaped by the political process and not primarily by analytic techniques. While agreeing that the resulting incrementalism (a process of making changes always within an already established program) in all probability will not result in complete success, they argue that through this approach successful efforts can be expanded and failures discarded.

How far should the planning function reach? If we believe, as proponents of pure rationalism do, that planning decisions can be reduced to a finite number of alternatives which are so distinct that a computer can indicate the appropriate choice among them, we are immediately faced with several difficulties.

It is very possible that different planners, investigating alternative solutions to a problem, could come up with different resolutions. In addition, unless the planner works in a society in which the causes of the problem and the desired program for relieving the problem are agreed upon, final decisions are made through negotiations among the competing interest groups. Problem analysis and intervention generation are inherently value laden. There are very few situations in which we find consensus about values so that planning can proceed solely on the basis of rationality.

Generally, it is felt that technicians should not be in charge. Rather planning is viewed as a political process in which planners introduce research and information and broaden the range of choices, and that will lead to an open climate for final decision-making. The politicians and citizens are presented with more than a single this-or-nothing choice. Planning by technical processes injects a more rational style into the traditional political environment.

TYPES OF TECHNOLOGY

Five major planning tasks or functions can be delineated, each with a supporting set of analytic techniques. The first is concerned with *assessing the state of the system or a specific group or population.*[2] More commonly, this is seen as the definition of the problem and the assessment of need. Under this general category are found tools of problem analysis, such as epidemiology (the study of the distribution and determinants of specific phenomena), and the analysis of organizational response in meeting social need (systems analysis, functional analysis, power-

[2] See, for example, Raymond A. Bauer, ed., *Social Indicators* (Cambridge, Mass.: MIT Press, 1966); Department of Mental Health, *The Application of Systems Technology to Community Mental Health* (Illinois Department of Mental Health, mimeograph, 1967); James March, ed., *Handbook of Organizations* (Chicago: Rand McNally, 1965); J. Reimer, E. Reimer, T. Reimer, "Client Analysis and the Development of Public Programs," *Journal of the American Institute of Planners*, 29 (November, 1963), p. 4; E. Shevky, W. Bell, *Social Area Analysis* (Palo Alto, Calif.: Stanford University Press, 1955).

influence analysis, and client analysis). These tools are useful in determining causation, need, and the capabilities of organizations as systems to achieve their ends. The techniques of social indicator construction and social area analysis (devices to measure the relative quality of life in specified functional areas and on an inter- and intra-metropolitan basis) and similar information collection techniques also fall within this general category of problem definition and need assessment. Finally, assessment of need would include survey research and the channeling of need and preference statements to decision-makers.

A second set of analytic techniques deals with *forecasting and prediction*.[3] Under this heading, a range of tools emphasizing a high degree of quantification have been developed as a direct result of the recent advances in the computer sciences and are based on linear programming and other multivariate statistical techniques (for example, trend analysis, input-output analysis, and probability analysis). Other methods not based on extrapolations and manipulations of data include the Delphi technique, future histories, and scenarios. The purpose of these techniques is the creation of a chronologically linked series of conjectured events which eventually form a "future environment," the development of a plausible series of events that might lead to the future state, and the examination of areas particularly sensitive to the final resolution or nonresolution of the problem and ways in which these areas can be modified.

A third set, falling under the category of *decision-making techniques*,[4] assist in resource allocation questions. The most popu-

---

[3] See N. C. Dalberg, *The Delphi Method: An Experimental Study of Group Opinion* (Santa Monica, Calif.: Rand Corporation Memo RM-5888-AC, June, 1969); T. J. Gordon, H. Hayward, "Initial Experiments on the Cross Impact Matrix Method of Forecasting," *Futures*, 1 (December, 1968), pp. 100–116; Wassily Leontieff, "The Structure of the United States Economy," *Scientific American*, 212 (April, 1965), pp. 25–35; Wolfgang F. Stolper, *Planning without Facts* (Cambridge, Mass.: Harvard University Press, 1966).

[4] See Freemont Lyden, Ernest G. Miller, *Planning Programming Budgeting* (Chicago, Ill.: Markham, 1967); L. Merewirtz, S. Sosnick, *The Budgets' New Clothes* (Chicago, Ill.: Markham, 1971); A. R. Prest, R. Turvey, "Cost-Benefit Analysis: A Survey," *The Economic Journal*, 75 (December, 1965), pp. 683–735.

lar of these techniques (in terms of recent literature) is Program Planning and Budgeting (PPB), which offers a comprehensive approach to decision-making through budgetary reform based on microeconomic analysis. Proponents of PPB view this as a mechanism to substitute rational comprehensive decision-making for the routines of incrementalism. While benefit-cost analysis is technically a component of PPB, its widespread application outside the PPB has resulted in its being accepted as a tool in its own right.

A fourth set of planning techniques could be described as the *service repertoire* which exists in different fields. What do we already know about intervention efforts in mental health, education, employment, and so on? What are the components of a specific delivery system or approaches to meeting needs in functional areas? What has worked in the past and what should be modified or expanded in the future? Included here would be all the information based on past experiences the planner will need to review in developing programs.

The final set deals with *evaluation* and includes such activities as monitoring (for example, time studies, cost analysis, quality control, communication systems for client feedback), impact analysis (for example, techniques to measure effectiveness and adequacy), and research design (for example, sampling, measurement procedures, and statistical analysis).

These five categories of analytic techniques are the repertoire of the planner and are supportive of the planning process, a process that is future-oriented, goal-finding, and concerned with problem-solving. The planner attempts to identify alternative courses of action and the consequences of pursuing each alternative. After selecting a particular strategy, results that are empirically detected are evaluated and program adjustments made. While the process itself is continuous, the analytic sets or subsets are discrete. Each has its usefulness and can make the process more rational, but each has limitations. Unfortunately, in practice, the tendency has been to select one set and to rely solely on its application, especially if the technique is proposed as a comprehensive system, such as Program Planning and Budgeting.

This chapter traces the development and application of two planning techniques that had initial widespread acceptance in the sixties—PPB as an experiment in decision-making, and evaluation, which has received more recent emphasis by the federal government. Our purpose is to explore the issues related to the use of technology in the planning process and the factors, both inherent and external to their application, that eventually led to their being discarded.

PROGRAM PLANNING AND BUDGETING— A STUDY IN TECHNOLOGY ABANDONED

PPB was one attempt at innovation that began with exciting prospects and ended in disappointment. The procedures used go back to the 1950s and military planning, but President Johnson's announcement in August, 1965, directing all major federal agencies to convert to a Program Planning and Budgeting System began the evaluation of its relevance for social planning. In the view of the prime movers of the Great Society, conventional budgeting had serious limitations. It was confined to a single fiscal year, thereby impeding any real examination of the future consequences of annual budget decisions. The existing budget process failed to specify program objectives or to review program accomplishments, and budgeting was conducted without explicit attention to the cost-effectiveness of alternative courses of action. While annual budget routines were useful for financing permanent bureaucracies and for making incremental adjustments in spending, they were not designed for charting major shifts in public policy.

Definitions of planning-programming-budgeting (PPB) or planning-programming-budgeting system (PPBS) seem to vary according to the background of the definer. It has been defined as systems-analysis, operations research, benefit cost analysis, marginal-utility analysis, program budgeting, and policy planning, to name just a few.

It is probably fair to say that PPB represented an effort at budgetary reform whose proponents hoped to substitute rational, comprehensive decision-making for the routines of incrementalism. Its major features include:

1. Identification of outputs for each service agency.
2. A systems analysis that identifies the inputs which are believed to be significant in achieving output.
3. The identification of costs for alternative combinations of inputs.
4. The calculation of a benefit-cost ratio for each combination of inputs and outputs.

"The crux of a PPB system is program analysis. The term 'program analysis' as used in a PPB system essentially consists of the process of determining the relative objectives, synthesizing alternative means towards these objectives, and identifying the costs and effectiveness (i.e., the 'benefits' or 'returns') of each alternative. Estimations of the costs for alternatives and the estimation of how the costs are likely to vary with changes in significant program characteristics are major parts of the analysis." [5]

As originally structured, PPB made use of informational incentives to reorient budgeting from a process of maintaining bureaucratic and spending continuity into an instrument for determining federal policy objectives. Through several special procedures, PPB was set up to supply planning and analytic data to policy-makers at key points in the budget-making cycle, and planning information was to be channeled through multiyear statements that projected the future costs and outputs of federal programs. A program structure would group together

[5] State-Local Finances Project, "The Role and Nature of Cost Analysis in a PPB System," PPB Note 6 (Washington, D.C.: George Washington University, April, 1967), p. 1.

all activities serving the same objective, making it possible to trade off among program substitutes, and provide a flow of analytic reports that would inform policy officials of the cost-effectiveness of policy alternatives. PPB took as an article of faith that, once exposed to analytic data, budget-makers would be stimulated to make more rational decisions.

The use of incentives to produce desired results is pervasive in American government and undergirds most intergovernmental grant and subsidy programs. But incentives do not always yield the intended effect because it is rare that the recipient is under the influence of a single incentive or a consistent set of incentives. The new incentive must compete with others, some of which are beyond ordinary governmental reach. Unintended spillovers from other programs as well as older, dominant influences can impede the effectiveness of many incentives. Moreover, past experiences often leave a legacy which cannot be eradicated quickly or painlessly. The bureaucrat newly armed with program data cannot easily write off client expectations whetted by previous budget commitments.

The way in which the program was begun, as well as its application in a system with unpredictable goals, influenced its eventual failure. PPB was launched across the board without prior testing or experimentation (though, of course, it was supported by years of Defense Department experience). It was anything but a piecemeal approach in that all major agencies and programs were covered. When PPB was started, confidence in its ability to liquidate hard-core social and human ills was ubiquitous in the federal government. During the high points of the Great Society, 1964 and 1965, scores of new programs—with promises of liberal financial support—sprang into being with little or no pretesting. Program planners were sure that they could rebuild cities, end poverty, bring educational opportunity to all. The problems would be as tractable in health care as in the construction of military hardware; the objectives as reachable in urban reconstruction as in space exploration. All that was required was the right combination of political will, program resources, and analytic know-how. The new analytic elite possessed an arrogance of intellect that is easy to caricature but difficult to recall. They could fine-tune the economy, specify in advance the cost and performance of a C-5A with contractual exactitude, predict what each incremental dollar would buy in lower mortality or accident rates. They were the answer men of American bureaupolitics, carrying their specialized skills and outlooks from the Department of Defense to the Department of Health, Education, and Welfare (HEW), to all government. The underlying philosophy was basically that where the solution is known or knowable, there is no need for deliberation. Full speed ahead is a reasonable, even a necessary, pace, and anything less robs the polity of the capability to produce at its "full employment" potential.

PPB was formulated during those years. It would be the system for buying the best answers through a reconstituted budget process that aimed for a future that past programs could not achieve. Of what value was all the analytic wealth if the budget preordained that last year's programs must continue and grow, if the future was mortgaged by past decisions? PPB was advocated (by the President) as the use of the most modern management tools to bring a finer life to every American at the least possible cost.

PPB turned out to be one of the closing episodes of the Great Society. By the summer of 1965, almost all the new programs had been formulated, much more the products of legislative frenzy than of analytic endeavor. Only weeks before PPB was announced, American ground forces took over responsibility for fighting in Vietnam and the black ghetto of Watts in Los Angeles exploded. When these separate events escalated to their awesome impact, America no longer was certain it had the answers. Nor did it have the money or the will for social innovation.

Thus by the time PPB moved from press release to budgetary realities, the conditions at the time of its inception had vanished. As the urban conflagration spread to additional cities, and the war on poverty settled for precarious tokenism, the market for bold systems analysis and long-range planning dried up. PPB was a system without users or uses, lacking both funds to support major new programs and incentive data about what works.

PPB did not succeed, at least in terms of reorienting federal budgeting. While it enriched the supply of program and analytic data, PPB did not uproot the incrementalist traditions of budgeting or turn the annual decision routines into an occasion for designing program changes. After several years of moribund existence, PPB was officially discarded in June, 1971, and while elements survive in some departments, especially Defense and Health, Education, and Welfare, nowhere does it exist with the salience and high hopes it attracted at the start.

The reasons PPB failed are complex.[6] It has been argued that it was grossly oversold and its contribution misrepresented by its proponents. Even if the successes claimed by the Department of Defense were real, it was somewhat presumptuous to state flatly these same successes would be realized in all governmental sectors. And yet it was natural to make these claims. PPBS to some extent proposes an oversimplified view of the world, that a given problem or goal can be encompassed by a specific set of objectives that are quantifiable or susceptible to pricing. While it is useful to apply techniques that assume a set of markets where items are priced and exchanged, some things cannot be priced or quantified. This, of course, opens up a series of difficulties. Who determines the objectives and how are values incorporated? Can values be expressed in economic terms alone? Finally, as discussed in Chapter 4, can we arrive at consensus points once we move down from broad statements of goals and objectives? The evidence indicates not.

We now seem to be in a new cycle, with emphasis on the an-

[6] For a detailed examination of possible reasons for failure, see Fredrich Mosher, "Limitations and Problems of PPBS in the States," *Public Administration Review*, 24 (March–April, 1969), pp. 160–167; Aaron Wildavsky, "Rescuing Policy Analysis from PPBS," *Public Administration Review*, 24 (March–April, 1969), pp. 189–202.

alytic aspects of PPB alone. Clearly PPB was too ambitious in its claim to be viewed as comprehensive planning technology meeting the wide range of needs throughout the planning process. Instead of its inherent value as a technique in decision-making functions, it *became* the planning process. However, even within this more limited view of PPB, it requires an explicit analysis across government programs, far more than any government structure is going to supply at any one time. The British system of program analysis and evaluation as a basis for decision-making offers an alternative to PPB. Analysis and evaluation are at the heart of each, but unlike PPB, the former appears to be a more acceptable strategy and in the long run more feasible.

Out of this experience with PPB, a number of conclusions can be drawn. The first is another reminder that a planning problem is not simply a technical problem that is dealt with under conditions of uncertainty. Rather in the more usual situation in which planning takes place, there is virtually no information about cause and effect. Second, PPB was not very well geared to consider distributional questions nor incentives in program delivery, two essential parts of our tradition. Finally, PPB, like most analytic techniques, cannot be seen as a substitute for the political process, as a replacement for negotiation. The contribution of these techniques is not so much in goal formulation nor in the selection of priorities, but rather in providing the basis for more rational decision-making by specifying choices and options.

While purely technical means of planning can be used for the distribution of hospital consultants, as Great Britain has done, and for school systems, the technical approach cannot be the sole process when dealing with matters of considerable social complexity. When problems such as unemployment are approached, you are forced to examine everything in society, including the whole politics of that society. Such problems are not technical in nature, and while technical knowledge can be helpful, they must be addressed as political problems.

EVALUATION AS A PLANNING TOOL

The recent emphasis within the federal government on the evaluation procedure can be viewed as a natural result of the decline of PPB. As the promises of the mid-sixties faded, we began to feel the need to document the experiences of the existing large-scale social programs—both successes and failures. Evaluation seemed a productive way for government agencies to spend an interlude in which program innovation was halted.

It is now clear that the first crop of evaluations only raised the level of confusion and pessimism. The Coleman Report on equality of education called into question the belief that had prevailed at least since the New Deal that education outcomes are substantially determined by the resources invested, and that the quality of schools, teachers, and facilities accounts for differences in student performance.[7] Instead, Coleman found that nonschool factors such as home and friends are more determinative. His appraisals of Title I compensatory efforts revealed that over-all additional spending does not uplift the disadvantaged, though some success stories have been reported. The Westinghouse review of summer Headstart programs reported that the benefits that are channeled into the brief, preschool experience fade away by the second grade. In a survey of educational research for the President's Commission on School Finance, a team of Rand authors examined a variety of approaches covering all major reform efforts.[8] These included the investment of additional resources, improving the processes and methods of education, variations in the organizational environment of the school, and large-scale interventions in education. They concluded that the interventions were not solving the problems in the educational field.

[7] James S. Coleman, Ernest Q. Campbell, Carol J. Hobson, James McPartland, Alexander M. Mood, Fredrich D. Weinfeld, Robert L. York, *Equality of Educational Opportunity* (Washington, D.C.: Government Printing Office, 1967).

[8] Harvey A. Averch *et al.*, *How Effective Is Schooling? A Critical Review and Synthesis of Research Findings* (Santa Monica, Calif.: Rand Corporation, December, 1971), p. xi.

The sense of failure among federal education specialists has also infected federal manpower programs, most of which are products of the 1960s and now are budgeted at about five billion dollars per year. Evaluation revealed that Work Incentive Program (WIN), Job Opportunities for Better Skills (JOBS), Coordinated Area Manpower Planning System (CAMPS), and an array of appealingly named projects have not materially closed the gap between disadvantaged and other groups. Blacks still have twice as much chance of being out of work and unskilled workers consistently have unemployment rates six times greater than those for skilled workers. These aggregate statistics undoubtedly mask the chronically high level of underemployment and withdrawal from the labor market among the poor. On balance, it is hard to take issue with the conclusion drawn from the Brookings study of the federal budget: "Manpower training programs in the 1960's also proved to be less successful than had been hoped. On the one hand, when unemployment was high, subsidized training programs in private industry tended to shrink, since employers were laying off workers generally. And in publicly run training programs, those who completed training could often find no jobs available. On the other hand, when unemployment was low, trainees were mainly the hardcore unemployed." [9]

Failure dominates the urban scene where an increasingly broad range of programs, beginning with public housing and now including urban renewal and Model Cities, have not restored vitality to the central city, nor even slowed the downhill trend. The first public-housing programs go back to the 1930s. It is now almost a quarter of a century since Congress legislated the goal of a decent home for every American, but we still are grappling with the problem of how to house the poor. Showcase public-housing projects, such as Pruitt-Igoe in St. Louis, opened in 1954 and already decaying and plagued with high vacancy rates, have been added to the old tenements as slum

[9] Charles Schultze *et al.*, *Setting National Priorities: The 1972 Budget* (Washington, D.C.: Brookings Institution, 1971), p. 198.

housing. Abandonment of buildings has become commonplace not only among slum landlords but among homes recently built or rehabilitated under Section 235 subsidies. Failure has been heavily concentrated in large cities where planning first gained a foothold in the United States. Nowadays, hardly anyone believes that the city can be saved by zoning, master plans, or even Model Cities.

Failure dominates the picture evaluation has provided of the impact of the Law Enforcement Assistance Administration. The streets are still unsafe and drug control programs have not halted the spread of addiction. On net, the welfare programs have not narrowed the income gap between the rich and the poor. A recent study sponsored by the Joint Economic Committee reported that the difference in income between the richest and poorest quintiles has almost doubled over the past twenty years. And on an individual basis, the earnings gap between technical and unskilled workers widened from approximately $3,800 to $6,500 during the 1960s.

With these reports of program failure, there appears to be a definite drop in interest in large-scale program evaluation, although many federal agencies are trying to institutionalize evaluation through the collection of output and performance data. Four factors are influencing the declining emphasis on evaluation.

The first is that most important evaluations raise a storm of methodological disputes. Social scientists and public officials are still arguing the validity and meaning of the Coleman findings. Mosteller and Moynihan,[10] summing up the main methodological complaints, state that the sample procedures were faulty and the nonresponse rate was too high. The number of school systems refusing to cooperate critically weakened final conclusions, and to expect school administrators to admit to inadequacies in their schools was certainly naive. It is no exaggeration to say that most major evaluations have been mired in

[10] Fredrich Mosteller, Daniel P. Moynihan, *On Equality of Educational Opportunity* (New York: Random House, 1972), p. 32.

similar controversy. While some of the difficulty might be mitigated by more careful measurement techniques, the main problem is that evaluators have not set the necessary conditions under which large-scale programs are evaluated.

For example, New York City increased by 30 to 40 percent educational expenditures to disadvantaged groups. Using the Stanford Achievement Test, evaluators came to the conclusion that the increased funds did not significantly increase the children's performance as the educators had assumed they would. The problem comes when the findings are interpreted. One could conclude that to change the school environment by increasing expenditures was meaningless. However, one could also conclude that the standard used to evaluate performance, the 1966 national medians, was inappropriate. In fact, if the 1953 medians had been used, roughly 75 percent of the pupils would have exceeded the standard.

Even with proper measurement one must still question the underlying logic of such evaluation. What is being tested, the management of a program or the impact of the program itself? Only when programs are managed as they were designed can we address the question of whether the underlying intervention theory—more educational resources to target populations—was in error. To jump from test scores to evaluating a theory is premature. A number of steps precede this conclusion. First, were the outcome measures sensible? Second, was there a difference between expenditures allocated and expenditures received? Unless you have input studies to determine whether in fact anybody received these funds, it is premature to raise the question of the program's failure, let alone the failure of the intervention theory. The failure might have been in the manner in which the programs were administered.

Evaluation is then potentially dangerous. Leaps are made which should not be made—from program outcomes to the theory of intervention upon which the program is based. In addition, accurate measurement procedures often lead to faulty conclusions. And yet, on the basis of evaluation, decisions are made to cut back or eliminate programs.

A second factor is that evaluation like PPB does not provide solutions. In terms of dealing with interventions to meet social problems, the evaluation often tells us only *what not to do*. Concerning the field of education, evaluative research has not revealed new approaches that offer substantial promise of significant improvements. If there had been more successes among the programs evaluated, the process might have provided the guidance needed for social change.

Another limitation, inherent in the evaluative procedure, is that cause and effect are often not so easily separated. For example, when infant mortality rates drop in a city, is the improvement due to Medicaid and other health programs, or to the liberalization of the abortion laws? Is the recent decrease in crime in some cities attributable to improved police surveillance, more effective courts, the expansion of methadone maintenance programs, or the migration of criminals to the suburbs?

The scope of the intervention can blur conclusions about its effectiveness. Current and past programs have usually dealt with only marginal changes, and many programs fail because institutional constraints prevent developing them with the scope necessary to produce any effect. Evaluation does not usually investigate this possibility.

Comparison of PPB and Evaluation

The problems of PPB and evaluation are quite different, and it would take a great deal of stretching to tie both failures to the same cause. One was tried and did not produce the expected results; the other was not given much of a chance. Yet the two cases offer some interesting parallels. Foremost is the fact that both techniques strove for change. PPB attacked the traditions of budget-making: the emphasis on workloads and line inputs;

the inflexibility of the fiscal year period; the neglect of program objectives and policy; and the rules and habits associated with incremental change. Because it is tied to the budget, PPB does not freely foster social change. The budget itself is a remarkable instrument for keeping bureaucracies in business, but it acts as a drag against change. Current commitments are favored over proposed changes, and increments available for new programs have been very small in recent years. Evaluation was seen as a way of destroying myths about program effectiveness and fostering innovation. As it turns out, evaluation can only tell us what does not work—it cannot generate new ideas.

Technology, as it is viewed today, is not particularly concerned with change and innovation. While this neutrality of technology is clearly the case within a pluralistic society, the view probably holds just as well if we were to move toward a nonpluralistic, central planning society. Its strength is really related to management and efficiency, and its basic concern is the evaluation of programs that were tried. Did they work and how successfully? Our experience with such tools as benefit-cost analysis and operations research has demonstrated that we now are in the position of making the same mistakes but more efficiently. In no way does their application constitute a reexamination of our basic posture on problem definition or analysis. There is a need to rise above a systems maintenance function. Technology as it is now applied does not lend itself to that basic step.

It seems that in the sixties we were proceeding on traditional wisdom in the areas of education, mental health, and manpower. It was very difficult to recognize in all the new approaches that we were institutionalizing new failures beside our old ones. Medicaid is a good example of this. In the early program design stage some of the negative results could have been predicted by putting it through a simulation model which would at least have predicted the direction price effects would take.

A second problem in the technological approach is related to the time frame required to evaluate social programs. In many cases, there is a tremendous pressure to conduct the evaluation and have the results available for the next budgetary process. Adequate analyses cannot, of course, be undertaken under these constraints and the tendency is either to discredit the process itself or to base decisions on preliminary and incomplete results.

The predominantly negative reports coming out of the recent flurry of evaluation procedures could be premature. The frame of reference that is used to evaluate programs is constantly shifting.

Jay Forrester, with little empirical evidence, has decided that there is too much housing in the cities and he is commanding a very respectful audience.[11] Evaluation, rather than refining the analysis of the problem, may simply lead to the abandonment of existing programs and a return to a very limited program of meeting housing needs.

Yet if the developments in Europe are analyzed, the process of evaluation should be a very long one. It takes a great deal of time, with considerable adjustment and changing of priorities on the basis of ongoing evaluation, if success is to be realized. Unfortunately in this country, planners and urbanists have little more patience than journalists or the public at large and are quite willing to act precipitously in throwing out programs. It may be that if extended the evaluative process would show that the program was not carried out on a massive enough scale to succeed.

A third limitation is that evaluative technology can threaten those in power—the government is unwilling to accept criticism. Even if we were able to resolve the methodological debate by more carefully evaluating whether the intervention theory was off target, or whether the program was administered effectively, evaluation is still likely to be suspect.

Is there a basic reason for politicians and administrators to

---

[11] Jay Forrester, *Urban Dynamics* (Cambridge, Mass.: MIT Press, 1969).

reject error, to reject being wrong, or is it possible to institutionalize means of error detection for positive reasons? Can we build monitoring and cybernetic steering into the planning-governing process so that past failure is a learning process?

There is a low failure tolerance in most governments, and it affects programs dramatically. The FHA is supposed to loan money to poor risks. If the agency loans money to such individuals, failures ensue, and the agency comes under attack by Congressional committees for mismanaging public monies. So instead, the original policy is subverted in practice to protect the agency, or is reversed outright. This is why Daniel Moynihan has played a particularly crucial role inside and outside the White House. He has claimed some success in national strategies because he sees the relationship between perceptions of success and government policy-making. It could be that many of the programs of the sixties would have turned out successfully if they had been allowed to continue. However, if the planners are forced to report failure because they cannot wait for results, or because the standards are changed when programs are close to success, they are bound to be ignored in the political arena. The political world is not geared only to reality, but also to perceptions of reality. Evaluation comforts those who do not want to spend more or embark on major program departures. Moreover, it usually is the risk-taking, innovative program that is subjected to evaluation—the ones most likely to fail—while long-standing programs avoid such rigorous scrutiny because of their greater familiarity and built-in constituencies.

Conclusions

While beginning with a broad definition of what planning technology entails, the major emphasis of this chapter has been on the specific techniques of PPB and evaluation. A number of conclusions can be reached.

1. Planning in a pluralistic society is dependent on the political process, and while technology is useful in identifying alternatives and tracing their consequences, it cannot replace negotiation and bargaining.
2. Technology has been shown to be useful in addressing questions of management and efficiency but has not demonstrated a capacity for stimulating innovation and change. Existing planning technology has been adopted for purposes that are totally inappropriate.
3. Finally, a series of planning techniques were identified that offer the possibility of overcoming some of the foregoing limitations. These include (a) the use of regulations by government to insure change, for example, regulatory functions currently used by FHA and FCC; (b) the development and institutionalization of social impact data, possibly modeled after the environmental impact statements, so that before a major domestic program could be funded, its impact on the poor and on poverty areas would have to be identified; (c) the use of incentives; and (d) broader use of simulation models.

CHAPTER EIGHT

MACHIAVELLI AND CELLINI: A DIALOGUE ON CENTRAL PLANNING[1]

If the various approaches to the subject of centrally planned change must be dichotomized, they may well be divided between a Machiavellian and a Cellinian view, so long as the invidious overtones which time has attached to the name Machiavelli are set aside. Machiavelli, often unfairly maligned, represents the knowledgeable expert who serves a Prince, or any master. Such a relationship may fairly be said to also describe the relationship between the modern-day expert who serves a leading political figure in Congress, the head of a major governmental department, or the elected executive of a state or nation. His efforts are defined by the power and the political requirements of his "master."

By contrast, Cellini is the artist, concerned with his own image of the world, who, nonetheless, enters sporadically into the political life of his time and may also succeed in changing the perceptions of leaders about the world around them, thus changing their course of action. However, Cellini lives his own life, outside of the constraints and shaping force of a particular

---

[1] The discussion is drawn from the final session of the Quail Roost Conference on Centrally Planned Change. The full names of the participants are listed in the back of this book.

government, bureaucracy, or of a particular "court"—he is not a part of an establishment, although he is a part of its world.

The following dialogue is introduced less to increase the polarization which has characterized the evolution of planning theory than to uncover certain promising views for continuous growth in theoretical perception which are summarized in the last chapter.

Gordon: I came looking for an answer to the question, "What is central planning?" And now that I have listened to planners, I have discovered that there is no single answer. I would say that central planning involves at least the following: a conscious ordering of social priorities and a decision to use public funds or a change in existing institutional arrangements in order to achieve those priorities.

Once the decision has been made to seek to achieve some of these goals or priorities, then four means might be used by the central government.

1. The government can appropriate funds, lay out a broad outline, and then turn implementation over to governments at a lower level. I gather that the community mental health programs fit into this category.

2. Or government can use something like a voucher system, providing maximum free choice to individuals, provided the money is spent to proceed toward the goals that have been delineated: education, health, or whatever. In this case, the market is being asked to create the supply to meet the demand that has been generated by the government vouchers.

3. In the pursuit of the goals that have been decided on, the central government can plan and then itself implement or administer the program. Social Security is a good example of this.

4. The government can seek to reach the selected goals by changing institutional arrangements.

In my own field, we can find several examples of my fourth alternative. The securities legislation in 1933 to 1934 completely changed the way that securities were sold, what was expected of securities dealers, what their liabilities were. It changed the nature of the banking system by divorcing commercial and investment banks. Another rather drastic change in institutional arrangements, dating back to the 1930s, was federal mortgage insurance which completely changed the structure of the housing market. The Federal Deposit Insurance Corporation, which for the first time gave us insured deposits and stopped the possibility of runs on banks, is another example. So too is the Wagner Act, which guaranteed collective bargaining and completely changed the nature of the relationship between labor and employers. And then, in the opposite direction, on welfare matters, the decision of the Executive Office of the President to move back toward a market system represents another attempt to change institutional arrangements.

Kahn: You are using the term institutional change in so broad a sense that almost anything would fit into it. In fact, there are finer distinctions to be made. Is it an institutional change to alter the incentive system by offering tax advantages or disadvantages?

Gordon: I agree the edges are very fuzzy. The case which I call institutional change can be called organizational change— you make it once for all. Once-for-all change affects organizational and individual behavior from then on. It may call for government supervision to ensure this change is maintained, as in the case of FHA, FCC, and the Office of Research and Development (ORD).

Donnison: Can we add a fifth means, which is the general influence government can exercise on the climate of opinion? What we have without this fifth mode is a categorization of the various ways in which government acts. We would have said nothing about planning. This is simply a way of dividing up the activities of government. There are many others.

Gordon: And you agree as to which of these types of government activity you choose and call them government planning?

Donnison: Governments do all four, and I would suggest five, types of things. The missing factor, it seems to me, is how one relates these different styles of action to each other. Governments do not choose between them; they have to do them all in one form or another.

Only if we relate these different styles of action effectively to each other can governments be said to have a plan or a program for the delivery of health services, or of education, or of highways, or of employment. The next step toward planning is to relate programs in different spheres of administration to each other. All governments are rather bad at that.

Barre: The distinction apparent throughout this discussion is that the word planning is associated with a set of systematic actions to induce a change in a way that the government is otherwise managing its activities, its programs. Otherwise, I don't believe there is a distinction. Apparently we identify—or the electorate identifies, or some significant portion of the government identifies—some dissatisfaction with the way the business of the public is being managed. We identify a set of goals for altering the way we manage, and then we develop some systematic way of altering it. It's that portion that we call planning.

Donnison: It is the sentence that Gordon began with, when he said "a conscious ordering of social priorities," that actually is the really important piece.

Gordon: Put it this way, the title of the conference is "Centrally Planned Change." The word "change" has just been brought up. Fit my classification in the following broader framework: an ordering of priorities that leads to the feeling of a need for change, and then the use of one of these categories to bring about that change.

Sundquist: It seems to me that there are three kinds of questions that are raised, and I don't know yet which one of them we are devoting ourselves to. Donnison is quite right in saying that these are five forms of governmental action or governmental intervention and not five kinds of governmental planning. I don't want to get into the question of semantics again. But the first question is whether there should be any governmental intervention at all.

Gordon: That's included. That is a change in institutional arrangements. If you decide to get the government out of the business, you're changing a set of institutional arrangements in which the people live.

Sunquist: Or conversely deciding to go into it. The first kind of question is the total scope of the governmental role in society. Then, given a decision for the government to intervene in a particular field, the second question is which of these four or five types of intervention is it going to use.

And the third question is the style. Within any one of these categories you've got a planning style which I think Webber explained better than anybody else. For example, you can have a style which is essentially nonplanning—which is random or careless, but has not qualified in the professional planner's terms as being real planning. You can talk about centrally planned change from any of those three aspects—scope, method, and style—and the choice needs to be made.

Gordon: I was just going to break in. A number of you may remember my welfare-function employment paper in which I spoke of national welfare conceived of by somebody as being a function of price change and level of unemployment. In other versions I've put in another variable which used to be extremely important in the United States. I expressed it by a fraction G/Y, the portion in the national income which should go to government expenditure.

A very important objective among conservative circles is that the role of government should be as small as possible. Now that could be one of your objectives, along with wanting to get certain other things done. Then you ask yourself, how do I combine these two objectives? The decision could be that you place highest priority on keeping the ratio of government spending to the national income as close to zero as possible. Then that obviously guides you with respect to all the other things you would like to achieve, how you go about doing them.

Pascal: I'm wondering whether some of the difficulty we are having in defining planning for social change is not due to the fact that we've been thinking about conservative marginal kinds of changes: a little more and better education; a little more day care than we now have. Therefore, we can't think of anything to do in terms of planning that's much different than we do now. Perhaps if we were to think of much more basic kinds of social changes it might raise in our minds interest in new planning devices that could be explored.

Let me offer a series of rather basic and fundamental changes—none of which I necessarily advocate—that seem to me to be radical and fundamental enough that they might call for these kinds of new planning mechanisms we're thinking about. One might be a redistribution of power relationships in the society in the direction of much more deconcentration, much more diffusion, and much more equality. Another might be to change the nature of work in such a way that you have the hope of a significant reduction in alienation, or significant reduction in the people's feelings of being locked into their jobs which could make work life much more variable. Another might be the conscious generation of alternative kinds of living styles, either in terms of size of place or part of the country, or family arrangements. If we think of social change in those more dramatic and fundamental ways, it might be that we would conclude that the kinds of tinkering and grant programs and vouchers and so forth that we had been considering are really not adequate or sufficient; that you have to go to some drastically new form of planning.

Wakefield: I have long thought of something along those lines—something like a national competition for alternative cities, wherein you would select different life styles which different people might like to adopt, various ways they would like to organize their lives. By competition we could develop three, four, or five different, physically structured, and institutionally organized cities. Then we would need to organize the mechanics of letting out the funds and the bidding and letting people opt as to which of these cities they would go to, and paying their way to get there. In other words, these would be really experimental cities. Those who wanted to live in a certain way and under a certain style of government could have choices.

Fisher: Well, that may very well be accomplished with a vast increase in available funds. I don't think it will get at the major existing problems in the metropolitan area. These problems are the biting and important ones. To me, centrally planned change has got to mean something about areawide direction of activities that occur in metropolitan areas. I think we can have incremental changes in different policies and programs for employment, income, housing, health care, day care, and so forth. It's how these things are delivered and manifested throughout the metropolitan area that requires major change.

One of the things that should be called for—and I think we had this just at the end of the Johnson administration—is some kind of a regional coordinator for each metropolitan area. We have to talk about a metropolitan development authority which would be comprehensive in terms of the kinds of tasks that would be performed, and which would be funded by the federal government. But it would have, through state powers, the authority to override some local decision-making.

Kahn: I want to get back to the issue of what planning is and stay away from any substantive illustration if I may. If you take Dr. Gordon's original schema, you're talking about some ordering of priorities and some decisions to use government power to realize it. Then David Donnison points out quite correctly that you can take this list and elaborate it a little bit and you have everything the government does. It seems to me that planning is in between those two steps, that is, between the decision to do the ordering, to choose the goals so to speak, and the decision to use public power or funds and sanctions to realize them.

The intellectual locus for planning is at that midpoint where one chooses the instruments with which public decisions are carried out. If you're taking a big target like Pascal is—institutional change is the goal of planning—then some instruments might work. And if you're taking a more modest goal like the delivery of one kind of service, some other instruments might work. The heart of the nature of planning is the way in which you decide what instruments to use. Sometimes you decide those instruments by conquest, sometimes by intuition, sometimes by crowd plebiscite, and sometimes by planning. The question of what is planning has to deal with what social instruments belong in that space between a goal choice and a decision to use public power. There are instruments that have something to do with specifying value parameters or what you're willing to take on in light of your important values. Other instruments have to do with what's going to work.

I would place the planning task at the point at which you choose the instruments and the way in which you choose to interrelate the instruments to use government power to realize chosen ends. In Dr. Gordon's paradigm, it's a big jump from conscious ordering of priorities and decisions to use public power to picking a list of instruments.

Gordon: Do I understand you correctly? You're saying that planning is planning how to plan.

Kahn: No, planning is choosing *how* to act to achieve certain goals.

Dyckman: It is a very easy extension of the comments you just made to the notion of meta-planning as Dror uses that term. As many of us have been concerned for a long time, the problems of organizing planning, organizing the system of planning, are a much more difficult and interesting task than the actual planning in the simple cases when the priorities are already determined.

That's really the harder question. In that respect I've been working backwards from one example toward the conclusion that the most difficult and interesting of all the planning tasks is to write a constitution. It requires all the technical knowledge that you have about the repercussions and the feedbacks that are likely to result in many areas. It also requires that you design a system, a social system, which will have the force of law, by which you have to prescribe the degrees of administrative freedom to make any other kinds of decisions.

I'm surprised that planners haven't more often considered this very ambitious task. It may be just an intellectual exercise—designing a constitution—or it may really be an art.

Because I was interested in this question for a long time, I read again the accounts of the great Philadelphia Constitutional Convention to see retrospectively what techniques people used when they were engaged in such a tremendous set of planning exercises. Of course, what they used was a series of extraordinary bargaining sessions in which trade-offs were made. But nobody wrote these down, and nobody now can reconstruct the actual trade-offs that went on in that remarkable hot summer in Philadelphia. That is to say, we can't reconstruct them exactly from the minutes of the Constitutional Convention. I'm sorry we can't because I've always felt we need a really good case study in how constitutions are written. If we could design a case, we could develop a game of writing constitutions, the most ambitious and extraordinary kind of game imaginable.

Donnison: There are four propositions that I'll try to elucidate briefly. First, we should always be very cautious—suspicious is perhaps not too strong a word—of talk about planning which starts from words like "comprehensive," "over-all," "life styles," "general constitutions," and "long-term strategies." To start there is to tackle the most difficult things first—things which call for the most detailed knowledge about the most complex range of situations relative to needs and the most complex relationships within government. It's rather like trying to go to the moon before we have built a bicycle.

So let us always start by choice with one program at a time, aimed at rather simple human needs, like stopping people dying, and making sure that they are adequately housed and fed, and so on. At the same time, let us always try to relate one program to another. We do indeed need to be comprehensive, we do indeed need to have an over-all look at our problems, and we are indeed building a constitution as we go along. But these things are to be done rather as wise men talk to each other and try to understand the world in which they live.

We should neither reject incrementalism nor willingly accept it when we can do better. We should recognize that we have to resort to it often, and yet we should always try to do better.

We should use all five modes of government action and all of them together. I want particularly to stress the fifth, which always tends to be forgotten—that is, changing attitudes and ideas, and formulating new assumptions; what we nonprofessionals generally call political leadership. If you look at the long history of British attempts to control the cost of living and the rise of wages since 1939, probably the most successful phase of that is the most derided of all—when Stafford Cripps spoke to the nation in 1948 and convinced people by sheer force of personality. There are many examples of this sort of climate setting by politicians. In a complex fashion, that is what has been happening in race relations in this country over the last decade.

Gordon: Under the Kennedy and Johnson administrations we called that jawboning.

Donnison: But may I add it isn't just bullshit. Neither will it work for long unless based on reliable information and cogent ideas. One of the more disturbing things about our conversation here is the lack of hard data and new information about society and the way in which it works. Without more information—genuine, relevant knowledge that people did not have before—we're not going to alter anything.

If you look at the changes which have occurred in Britain in attitudes about capital punishment and the organization of secondary education, you can actually identify almost to the month the point at which the balance shifted—the point, for example, at which the defenders of capital punishment had to start making their case first instead of waiting to respond to their opponents. And that was due partly to information—the continuous repetition of information about the effects of hanging people. The fifth mode of intervention is not just jawboning but the employment of actual knowledge and hard data. This point is addressed particularly to us in the academic community upon whom the country relies for information and critical analysis.

Morris: That's really a very interesting approach, the idea that a hard, persistent effort, learning piece by piece, will in itself contribute to the changing of public attitudes—to building consensus.

Niskanen: We have had difficulty with the concept of planning, but I think that it might be useful to distinguish two polar images of the planner. One image which most of the group here seems to share is the planner as either a decision-maker, somebody who structures a decision process, or who is an advisor to the leader, a Machiavelli to his prince. Another quite different image is of the planner as an artist, a Cellini, who poses unperceived or poorly perceived alternatives to present arrangements, who has an image of conditions that he makes known in the form of models of various kinds. In some cases they are physical models, in some cases they are drawings, or in some cases they are literature. That model of the planner as Cellini rather than Machiavelli is a model that is closer to conceptions of the city planners—somebody who poses interesting alternatives to the way the things are happening at the present time.

Those who think of planning as an art are likely to be very much less frustrated than those who see it as a part of the political system. I think it's more realistic. And it's a model that a wide range of political persuasions and wide range of persuasions about the process of government all could accept. Needless to say, it's a model which most appeals to me.

Sundquist: I'd like to return to an opening remark by Morris about one of the motivations for this conference—that planners seem to be demoralized and need to get together and shore one another up.

I'm reminded that back in 1933 the government engaged in a massive intervention in the economy designed to end unemployment—or at least drastically reduce it—and end the depression. We had a pump-priming program and other forms of intervention beginning in 1933 that extended for a half-dozen years. Along about 1939 things were not really any better and the conservatives hopped on the interventionists and said this proves that government planning, government intervention, doesn't work. But then, in 1940, we started to rearm, and in 1941 we really had pump-priming on a massive scale, and we did end unemployment. We brought it down to practically zero. Government intervention in the economy turned out to be a huge success. What that seemed to prove was not that governmental intervention was wrong, that government planning was bad, but that it hadn't been done on a massive enough scale.

Now we're in the same position, it seems to me, on social planning. We had a kind of 1933-type crescendo in the 1964 to 1965 period. We launched the war on poverty and started out on an urban program and went forth with Model Cities and the whole battery of 400 other categorical programs. Five years later people are saying: it didn't work, planning is a failure, government intervention is a failure. I wonder if it isn't the same kind of situation, where the answer is that we didn't have intervention on a massive enough scale. For the intellectuals to get together and say planning has been discredited by the experiences under the war on poverty and the Great Society is probably a great mistake.

We don't really know whether these programs worked or not. From the evaluations I've seen, some did and some didn't. Community action programs succeeded in some respects and failed in others. There is a tremendous opportunity to sort out the successes from the failures and decide where to go from there. I think Logue would tell us that urban renewal, which has been a very aggressive intervention in the economy, has worked in enough respects that it's worth building on and developing and using more often. I expect the same is true in other programs as well.

But the ups and downs of governmental intervention and

governmental planning are part of the political process. That's what the political debate in this country is really all about—insofar as there's a division between the parties, the split is precisely on this issue. It developed in the 1930s when the Republican party took the position: go slowly because if we do things will right themselves—intervention will have worse side-effects than if we don't do it at all. The Democrats responded with the demand that the government move in. This issue has arisen in one form or another in every subsequent campaign.

By 1968, the interventionists lost the election and the conservatives won. We're meeting now in the intellectual atmosphere created by the fact that a conservative administration is in power. Now there isn't the difference between parties on this question that there was thirty years ago, or even twenty years ago, or ten years ago. But there still is a difference. If you don't believe that governmental planning has worked, it's partly because we're in a position where the government has withdrawn a considerable amount of support from the whole idea of intervention. Where there is intervention, the government has tended to withdraw support from the kinds of intervention that involve more rather than less governmental activity.

Gordon: If I understand you, you can't be a planner unless you're a registered Democrat.

Niskanen: The Sundquist argument that one should neglect the information developing in the short run when things aren't working too well—that one must have faith to keep doing something long enough and on a scale large enough and everything will work out—reminds me of two arguments, one facetious and one real. One is the response of the retailer who said "I lose a little on every item, but make it up on volume."

The other response is not at all facetious. It's exactly the same argument that was made with respect to the Vietnam war. Every month things looked bad and developing information looked like it was getting worse. The argument of the military was, yes, we admit that the bombing hasn't worked out but we've got to bomb longer and we've got to bomb harder and we've got to bomb new targets; don't bug me for five years, and then later, ten years. First they wanted 100,000 troops, then they wanted 500,000 troops. Finally, they asked for a million troops and it was turned down. I think people who propose that the body politic stand still for periods longer than the natural rhythm of American political life, which is four years, are unrealistic and, in some sense, very dangerous. They suggest that we put our trust in them and that, somehow, we'll come out at the other end of this long, dark tunnel, but led through it by people who know more or who are somehow wiser than we are. I find that I would not want to live in a society in which that was the general practice.

Sundquist: I accept at this point that belief in governmental intervention is in a large part an article of faith. But I think it applies equally to the other side of the argument; to be against governmental intervention is also an article of faith that the social ills will somehow correct themselves without governmental action. In the absence of much rational proof on either side, it becomes a gut kind of issue. As I said, it's the heart of politics. Some have more faith here and some have more faith there.

Niskanen: My argument is not an argument for or against planning; it is an argument for marginalism; it is an argument for paying attention to marginal changes and to developing signals. And, in some sense, that is much more characteristic of the American approach toward things than either planning or nonplanning.

Sundquist: If you had paid attention to signals in the thirties, where would that have led you?

Niskanen: It probably would have kept us out of a lot of mischief.

Sundquist: I mean, would it have led you to more spending or less spending?

Webber: You're in effect equating governmental intervention with planning. You're using the terms interchangeably. I want to make a distinction, as several others here do, too. The issues that are troubling us are those that command governmental attention. And it may be that, in some instances, governmental intervention is the right way to do it, but in some instances it may be that privatization is the right way to do it. Planning is a technique for finding means that work better, accomplishing whatever it is we're trying to accomplish. We should experiment and try to find out what happens after we've acted interventionally or privately.

Planning has these four characteristics: examination of alternatives, projection of their consequences, monitoring their outcomes after the fact, and evaluation of the outcomes. The question is not are we for or against governmental intervention—that seems to me to be irrelevant. What we're trying to accomplish are some social changes which public spending may or may not help, depending upon the nature of the system that we're dealing with. Our hang-ups are that we don't know very much about the way these systems work, which is what Donnison was saying; we're too ignorant. We tend to turn toward doctrinaire positions or preferred styles of action, like spending or not spending, or child care or not child care, community health centers or centralized health centers. Until we have the analytic equipment that permits us to use these public actions as experiments, in effect, we're not going to learn very much.

Rein: I find this discussion very interesting. Webber has told us throughout the conference that planning is really learning through experience that allows us prior information that can inform us as an advisor and as a result of which we are better able to make a choice.

And then I look at the discussion between Niskanen and Sundquist. It's very clear one starts with a belief system, a creed, a set of loosely organized ideals, and then confronts evidence which each uses for quite different purposes. What shall we, in fact, learn from the decade of experience during the sixties? What's the lesson? The lesson depends clearly upon the nature of one's belief system. And we have two very different postures. Sundquist is convinced that government is a good thing and we should have more of it; and when it fails, it is because of lack of faith in government. Donnison has been telling us this as well. But Niskanen draws exactly the opposite conclusion.

First premises are essentially creeds and belief systems. Surely the question must be, do we take all information and relate it back to our first premise, to our belief system, or do we ever in fact modify our belief system in any sort of fundamental way? This would seem to me to be what learning might in fact be about. It's very clear that most dialogues and debates and discussions about the use of evaluative research simply use information to assimilate a belief which has been arrived at on quite different grounds.

Morris: It's interesting to speculate whether or not there is a common ground being approached between Sundquist and Niskanen. Those committed to government intervention on the massive scale are beginning to think of selectivity rather than universality, whereas those on the other side are recognizing that you can't just leave problems alone, that you have got to have some government intervention. The Nixon administration is a good example; it *is* intervening in some ways.

Dyckman: It's worth distinguishing when considering the question of marginal versus large-scale change, whether, indeed, in parts of the system at all times you don't have to make rather large changes. That is to say, one might use all the information given by a system in terms of the marginal effects indicated, and still make the decision that within a program scope, or to achieve a particular objective, he's going to have to make some very large commitments. If you were to consider only marginal interventions there are many kinds of things you could not do at all.

For example, it is very clear that you can undertake a program like building new towns—a program which maybe we ought not to do—and make it work only if you do it very big. This is one of those relationships on which a lot of evidence is coming in. If you compare Brazilia with Ciudad, for example, their success or failure is largely a function of scale and resources that were put into them. In the case of Brazilia, they put in enough. A new town, with a half-million people, turns out to have a much better chance of success than one with 200,000. The question of scale becomes a critical factor in many programs. I would not like our general respect for the informational value deriving from marginalism to blind us to the fact that there are appropriate sizes for many kinds of programs. It may very well be that in the case of social programs this is also true.

There is one final lesson that was suggested by the Vietnam war analogy: that is, if the program is a bad program to begin with then you ignore marginal signs at your peril. It may be, of course, that the military was right in one respect. If they were going to succeed at all in the hopeless venture, they had to do it very big. But the venture itself may have been hopeless, and that's quite a separate issue.

There is even a scale in the planning activity itself—this scale includes a time scale. One of the virtues of long-range planning is *not* the literal guidance system which long-range planning would provide. Quite the contrary, it always fails to provide such literal guidance. The beauty of long-range planning is that it better informs *present* decisions. It allows you to see a few more things that you have to take into account now, and that is really the only redeeming virtue of it. There is a type of scale factor in the planning operation.

Logue: I'm troubled about the direction this discussion is taking. I think most of us would agree that marginalism is the system that we operate under in this country. We've talked about centrally planned change without giving an example that we might focus on.

There is one interesting example—very important to the society: can we, through centrally planned change, eliminate racial discrimination and inequality in this country? That is the most important thing about this country today. We pick at it quite marginally and, if centrally planned change is to have any meaning, it would be interesting to find out whether a group of social scientists from all the various disciplines that are here could indicate how it can apply to this subject.

I don't think we've been using the word planning properly. Planning, to me, means that you think very carefully in alternative ways about what you want to do and why you want to do it, and how you want to do it. But most things in government don't happen that way. They just happen. It would be interesting to construct in this group an ideal educational system, health system, welfare system, employment system, or housing system; or even to derive ideal policies for population distribution. If you focus on something like that as the aim of centrally planned change, you could have a useful discussion. But, as I listen around the table, I hear that centrally planned change can be for anything at all—of great importance or of no importance.

Rein: Most people would be delighted if we could figure how the hell we do any one of those things; we'd pay almost any price to get this over with instead of just passing on a bad situation in a marginally improved way to our children, which is what we're doing now.

Frieden: I think that is what is implicit in Logue's suggestion and also in Webber's conception about planning as learning through experience. It is the need for some kind of consummated commitment that goes beyond the commitment to a single specific program. If some of the fields in which we were active in the 1960s were seen as a part of the continuing responsibility and ongoing function of government—say, a deep concern about closing the income gap between the poor and the rest of society—then the failure of a single program would not be a fatal blow to us. We'd be prepared to look at shortcomings in programs and make changes while working toward that goal.

The Vietnam war analogy is not a good one. The war on poverty itself is not a good one, if one thinks of that as a battle that can be won through some concerted plan of action in a fairly short time. The question of the continuity of commitment gets to the distinction that Niskanen was drawing between the two styles of planning, Machiavelli versus Cellini. Cellini can flourish where there is some kind of ongoing consensus that attention needs to be paid to a problem and ideas are needed. But where consensus itself is wavering, the planner himself has to get into that role of trying to build his own support as he goes, which can also be very destructive to any kind of ongoing planning. Where you have that consensus and where there is the institutionalization of some ongoing function of government, then a planner can reasonably work as a technician, as a bureaucrat, as a designer of programs.

We find ourselves partly in that role as technician, or partly in the role of trying to attract attention and build consensus to create conditions in which planning can happen.

Many of the programs which have now taken very serious blows may suffer from the fact that it takes so long to gather support for a program. By the time a program becomes operational, the reality assumptions on which it was based no longer hold true. Most of that was true in the case of urban renewal. At the time some of the elements of that program were first conceived, just before and just after World War II, those assumptions might have worked fairly well; but when those assumptions were applied to the cities of the late 1950s, with race problems and housing shortages, and high construction costs, it didn't work well any more. On the other hand, with the wholesale abandonment of many entire neighborhoods in cities, urban renewal might fit better into the context of the late 1970s than into the 1950s and 1960s.

Morris: Do we know how to construct an approach that will significantly cut into inequality? Or if we don't know, are we then searching for some way which will assure us the continuity of commitment which will build up the capacity to know how?

Webber: That is really the sort of question I would like to put to us, too. Maybe one formulation of it is how come in America we've never tried to do this? How come it's always so *ad hoc?* Why is it that we're always grabbing at programs as though those were the salvation or the road to salvation? And it's all very partial and lumpy and we haven't tried to confront inequality per se. We tried community action or housing with short experiments and not enough time to run out the effects or without the monitoring to know whether they worked. Why is it that in America we haven't had the mind set that asks us to take on a long task? The Fabians were really of a different sort—this may not be a good comparison. They had a large policy set that they were trying to attack, and deliberately went out to create a governmental apparatus over a prolonged period of time with lots of different efforts to attack the problems of inequality. But in America we haven't done that.

Sundquist: We have. The war on poverty used all of the planning techniques known as of 1964 that could possibly be used. They had the best economists in the field. They analyzed the problem in terms of preventing entry into poverty, expediting exit from poverty. What else can you do?

Niskanen: We had an awful lot of good analysis done, but that was independent of the programmatic action. The evaluation, the analysis, almost completely paralleled the nature of the programmatic development, but there was very little touching between these two streams.

Sundquist: Planners came out with seventeen or eighteen specific means to the end, and most of those were adopted and a few were added.

Webber: Did that include trying to do something about varying the national economy?

Sundquist: O yes! The tax cut of 1964 was part of the plan and it went through as scheduled down to the exact dollar figure.

Logue: There was a time—and it stopped maybe twenty years ago—when we had centrally planned policy to preserve racial inequality. We did a pretty damn thorough job of it.

Donnison: But it was not planned. Most of it conflicted with the things that every American child by the age of eight could reel off for you about being an American.

Logue: It would be wrong to say that it was not a policy. It was a policy.

Donnison: It's only a policy in a sense that a lawyer looking at a massive variety of decisions might discern precedents. It's sort of *post hoc.*

Webber: It's an implicit policy.

Rein: What we have come to in the last part of the discussion is the relationship between consensus and planning. It is very clear that there is a disagreement, and a very important one, which goes back to first principles, although we have not yet decided where these first principles come from. We could turn to Logue's question about equality and whether that is an important national priority, and discover quickly there would be disagreement about whether we would in fact promote equality of conditions or only equality of opportunity—and what we mean by equality. We will discover that there is no consensus. Then clearly we will say we have got to stop that exercise because we can't make any progress if we are going to disagree on first principles, and that we must get on to planning.

So, I want really to raise this question: what is the form that planning takes when, in fact, it must always proceed without consensus of commitment or purpose, without consensus with respect to the instruments of the intervention—because the means of intervention themselves form an ideological debate as important as the debate about equality itself. Planning has proceeded with this fundamental ambiguity.

Niskanen: My point is much the same as Rein's. The reason why we typically pursue a programmatic approach rather than a wholesale national commitment to a goal, the approach that Logue may be suggesting, is that we don't have that consensus on a goal. The characteristic of effective political entrepreneurs is that they are capable of putting together program ideas which serve a sufficient multiplicity of goals to achieve a sufficient consensus on programs or on instruments, not necessarily on a goal. One of the reasons why evaluations are difficult in public policy-making is that a characteristic of evaluation is to select one of these perceived goals and then to evaluate the programs against that goal. In actual fact, the necessary coalition to achieve approval of an instrument includes people who support it for quite different reasons, and who are unprepared to see that instrument or that program evaluated on one of the several goals of those people who support the program. I don't see any way out of that impasse. It will continue to be the case as long as we rely—and I hope we continue to do so—on consensual government.

Rein: I find a fundamental conflict between evaluation and these political purposes for putting things together. That is what the tension is, in fact, about.

Sundquist: Using Niskanen's distinction between Machiavelli and Cellini types of planners, what happens is that each side gets its own Cellinis. When there is a change in administration, the planner types change. Each administration has its own economists. Walter Heller could not work for the Republican administration and Herbert Stein could not work for the Democrats because they did start from different first principles. I remember in 1946 the Congress passed a legislative reorganization act and they said we were really going to put science and planning at the service of both parties without regard to the party. These people should be above politics. So they established a professional staff for all committees.

By this time, there isn't one that has a professional staff left. Both sides discovered they just weren't useful for their purposes. They had to have planners who would come in with statistics which would be sound, accurate, proper, well analyzed, but would essentially support their point of view. As we get consensus of society we push back considerably the area of disagreement. But you never push it all the way back, and there is still a huge realm where decisions are made without the benefit of the kind of planning you are talking about.

Rein: And that's what makes Webber's model incomplete.

When he says "learn from experience," he leaves out these very critical first principles which could help you organize that experience, and which do not seem to be subject, in any sort of fundamental way, to information itself.

Niskanen: I learn from that the glass is half-full, you know, and he learns that it's half-empty.

Rein: I tried to pin Fred Hayes down about what lesson he learned from the expenditure for education in New York City. It's very clear that there are two very different lessons. One lesson that could be learned is that it was a bad thing to do, and government ought to get out of the business. Or, you can learn just the opposite lesson; we didn't commit ourselves long enough, hard enough, sustained enough, with broad enough scope, to make the thing really work. What lesson do you learn from that? I don't see how you can simply assert we learned from that experience.

Logue: Niskanen should come to know soon that all our first-rate planners are Machiavellis *and* Cellinis. But I think that Rein and Donnison know it's really not a satisfactory conclusion to say that you can't have long-term, large-scale, centrally planned change. The interesting thing about this country is that in the last twenty-five years probably the two most important changes were centrally *un*planned change: the mobility of an agricultural labor force which became technologically unemployed, and second, a national housing policy which is all but totally oriented toward all-white suburbs. The consequences of neither were foreseen because everybody was accepting your formulation that it's too bold, that you can't get a consensus, and, therefore, you will avoid it. But you must not ever think that there are no policies that do not make significant differences.

Moroney: It's interesting that in that last session we're coming down to one of the basic issues that has always been in my mind—the relationship between consensus and control. The whole question of consensus bothers me because we're talking about values, we're talking about dominating themes in society.

We have the view that somebody can feel the pulse of what the desires are and become very technical or Machiavellian and try to meet vested interests and to further whatever the desires of the society are. But if you do have some conflict or confusion about what the dominant themes are, how do you relate to Ed Logue's question about something above such petty interests? You can't do it. I don't think that we set up planners who are critics of the value system itself. This leads to elitism. This leads to some groups saying we are the critics and we know what is best for society even though the majority of people might not agree with us, and some how we are going to get enough power to do something about it. Who checks the elites; who checks the Ed Logue who is looking for equality?

Kahn: I think it's wrong to set up a dichotomy between the extreme incremental position and the position that says you can do big things. It's true you have to have value consensus and moral consensus around a lot of things. It's also true that we are somewhere along the way on some issues and not on others. At given moments of history, at given moments of trauma, we can get a moral consensus on some issues and go somewhat further. It's also true that there is such a thing as political leadership in this society, which, if you call it that, may be the same thing as elitism. Sometimes societies have political leaders who not only tap the moral consensus but also help shape it, say, Lincoln and Churchill.

As I reflect on this discussion, this should not have been called a conference on centrally planned change. The question of central or not central is not the issue. The issue is the degree of comprehensiveness and how large a bite to take. The issue is where to locate a particular act between marginalism and something more. Planning is at various stages along that continuum, depending on what it can buy at a given moment about value consensus and goal consensus. If it's true that Webber's moral doesn't make sense unless there is some continuity of goal, it's also true that a society can keep its view on some goals if it has leadership and if it discusses them and enunciates the issues.

Barre: I think there has been an exchange here which has brought us very close to the nub of the issue. I think Sundquist's set of comments imply that for any particular objective there is a scale of intervention required and the two must be conceived of together if a solution is to be achieved, rather than being conceived of in terms of degree of governmental intervention. Niskanen's conception of incrementalism tends to ignore Sundquist's idea of the necessity of having a scale of intervention for resolving a particular problem. Or else he is saying it is impossible to define problems precisely enough to organize our government or private forces to achieve a scale of major changes in relation to conditions seen as major problems. Therefore, he accepts short-range, smaller problems and works incrementally.

Logue offered us two excellent examples of what he referred to as sequences of nonplanning which make changes in the society. Donnison has advocated focusing on single systems of intervention because of the complexity of trying to achieve a large or a complete alteration. We are now evaluating Logue's two policies in a context different from that for which they were created. The agricultural policy did not pay any attention to inducing an alteration in the location of the population. It was a policy of a single system that Donnison referred to, although he did caution us to be aware of the interaction of that system with other systems. Maybe so, but we weren't aware of this. We did, through agricultural policy, achieve all the objectives of that agricultural policy well over a period of a generation at least. But it has caused problems that might have been recognized had we approached the over-all problem of national organization on a scale that maybe Sundquist could have accepted.

The illustration on housing leads to the same conclusion. The FHA did achieve its purpose. It did create a fiscal system which yielded six to eight million houses. Its purpose was not addressed to where those houses should be located when the system was created. Again, go back to the single system mode of attack. It was done at a time when this society was trying its hardest to be aware of how to change itself and how to anticipate the alternative effects of our policies, in 1934 and 1935. But it was a single mode of attack and the secondary effects of having achieved that objective were not considered, were not visualized in time. It joined with some other forces which have created the major alteration of our metropolitan areas. Now somewhere in here is the tie between incrementalism and scale of problem necessary to find a purposeful plan.

Rein: I would like to end the conference with a question to Niskanen and Sundquist taking off from Webber's formulation. If planning means really learning from experience, but the experience deals with views which are passionately held and which one has political stakes in, then I would like to know what kind of information would ever change your view that we need less government or change your view that we need more government? Is there any information that would in fact get you to change your views?

Niskanen: It is a characteristic of centrally planned change that it leads to both more dramatic successes and more dramatic failures. The most dramatic of the two polar extremes in the 1960s is the Apollo program and the Vietnam war. The choice between whether one generally prefers centrally planned change to incrementalism, I suppose, is answered by whether one values the potential successes more than he fears the potential losses.

But let me conclude on an intellectual point rather than a specific programmatic problem. The way to close the loop on Webber's model is the Kuhn model of the theory of scientific revolution.[2] For most people, most of the time, learning from experience means reinforcing their existing paradigm, as, it is quite clear, Sundquist and I have done. It takes a truly massive accumulation of evidence to get people to change their paradigm. One of the differences between the United Kingdom and the United States in the 1960s is that some of us saw a truly massive accumulation of evidence which changed some of our

[2] Thomas S. Kuhn, *The Structure of Scientific Revolutions* (Chicago, Ill.: University of Chicago Press, 1962).

paradigms. I worked on MacNamara's staff before the Office of Management and Budget (OMB) and I was part of the whole system analysis unit serving the prince role. You don't achieve this change of paradigm either on an individual basis or a social basis in the absence of a truly massive accumulation of evidence. The great depression was a condition which changed a lot of people's paradigm. The Vietnamese war has caused a lot of people in the United States to search for a new paradigm. But you shouldn't expect the drifts of evidence to change the paradigm itself—it will usually lead to reinforcing the paradigm.

CHAPTER NINE

PERSPECTIVES AND PROSPECTS

We return to the theme with which this book began: what has been the experience with centrally planned change in America? What are its prospects as a model of societal guidance in the future? A wide range of perspectives on centralized planning based on governmental efforts in the fields of urban development, employment, and mental health have emerged from this volume. Two models, planned decentralization and the use of market mechanisms, were examined in light of their capacity to achieve social goals. Do these many perspectives reflect irreconcilable views about the nature of planning, or is each only a variation of a kaleidoscopic subject? Are the alternative models of governmental intervention antithetical to or consistent with the concept of centrally planned change?

In this concluding chapter an attempt will be made to answer these questions synthesizing the discussions in earlier chapters and pointing to some prospects for further development in planning theory.

ALTERNATIVE PERSPECTIVES ON CENTRALLY PLANNED CHANGE

The multiplicity of perspectives reflected in discussions regarding the nature of centrally planned change leaves the impression of a field in conceptual disarray. For example, some seem to argue that centralized planning is at best a marginal activity effecting small incremental changes in existing policy to avoid disasters which may accompany large-scale interventions. We do not know enough, so the argument goes, to redesign a system in its entirety, nor do we have sufficient consensus for doing so. Therefore centralized planning must be gradual in nature, a step at a time placed on a well-laid foundation. A contrary view is that marginal or piecemeal efforts prevent centrally planned change. Central planning requires a basic restructuring of the system, a change in institutional arrangements, or a reordering of priorities. Unless the intervention is massive, no significant results are achieved.

There are also differences over whether thought or action should be the primary mode of planning. Some people argue that planning is essentially the identification of alternative courses of action to achieve some predetermined goal, anticipation of their respective consequences, and an evaluation of their relative merits. Others see planning as advocating action —a commitment to some objective by marshaling information in support of that objective, by pushing the boundaries of existing consensus, by leading the public to a recognition of issues and a new definition of goals.

It may appear that these divergent views can never be merged to build a model of centrally planned change. Indeed, the debate seems to question the very criteria used in Chapter 1 to delineate the nature of centrally planned change. However, further reflection reveals that these polarities are intellectual abstractions and do not represent the behavior of planners in reality.

The debate can be resolved on two grounds. In the first place, such positions represent first principles, or belief systems, not empirical representations of how the world works. They are truly "perspectives" from which the planner tries to understand and organize the world. To the extent that planners are pragmatists, they must ultimately subject the positions and programs of these perspectives to the crucial test: how well do they reflect reality? First principles or belief systems may be modified or discarded when programs developed on a premise have failed. In the face of repeated failures or inconclusive results, the planner will move from either his marginal or massive view of social intervention.

Second, such abstract positions can be reconciled in the context of a particular problem. The scale of intervention chosen—incrementalist as opposed to massive—has more to do with the nature of the problem situation than with the mode of planning one favors. Some systems are highly sensitive to alterations and small-scale interventions are appropriate, while in other situations massive intervention may be required to achieve significant results. The scale of the intervention must be appropriate for the problem being addressed.

Thus nothing inherent in these varying perspectives invalidates the concept of centrally planned change. Rather these perspectives indicate the variations necessary to make centralized planning work in different times, in different places, and with respect to different problems.

The model of centrally planned change proposed in this book has four dimensions: (1) universal in its application, (2) empowered with resources to achieve goals, (3) developmental in its time context, and (4) redistributive in its effects. Such a model of planning is by its nature highly centralized and often has been equated with administrative or bureaucratic planning in the sense that decisions are made at the top of a hierarchy and specific actions are implemented by command down through the decision structure. The models of decentralization and market-based planning are marked departures from such a conception, but not inherently inconsistent with our four dimensions of centralized planning.

Decentralization and the use of the marketplace for the delivery of public goods are disaggregative approaches to societal guidance. They both require in essence a common interest on the part of the disaggregated units, whether they be consumers in the market or residents of a political subdivision. This common interest is achieved either by some external control that establishes such units, that is, all persons with the same interests are assigned to a given decision-making unit; or through some choice mechanism by which individuals select their decision-making unit on the basis of shared interests; or through the creation of some functional unit by which people are grouped around a single or interrelated tasks. Such homogeneity is essential in order to assure that disaggregated units function adequately from a larger societal point of view. Examples of such disaggregation discussed in this book are the Tiebout model of suburban government, borough government in London, worker-governed enterprises in Yugoslavia, and the voucher/ market system for the provision of public goods.

There are three types of activities which such models cannot accommodate: (1) the provision of public goods which cannot be disaggregated, such as police protection and transportation; (2) the distribution of resources among the disaggregated units; and (3) the management of externalities among units. The assurance of public safety cannot be maintained unless there is some kind of uniform program throughout the self-contained system. A transportation system is impossible since arteries pass through more than one disaggregated unit. Any attempt at redistribution requires some degree of centralized control over public financing. Some form of centralized constitution or rule-making is necessary in order to establish the rights of individuals operating in that system as well as their responsibilities vis-à-vis the welfare of others.

These three functions clearly call for centralized decision-making and implementation. They are completely consistent with the four dimensions of centralized planning as outlined above. But such planning need not be administrative-bureaucratic in nature. It involves a different style characterized by (1) the use of incentives or supplements to induce disaggregated units to produce certains goods, (2) the evaluation of such investments to see that public objectives are achieved, (3) the specification of privately provided public goods through contracts that assure public objectives, and/or (4) the establishment of rules and sanctions that can be applied to protect the rights of individual units. Although decentralization and the use of the market are clear alternatives to administrative-bureaucratic planning, they can be considered variations of centrally planned change.

PROSPECTS FOR THE DEVELOPMENT OF THEORY AND PRACTICE

In this book we have addressed the notion of centrally planned change from the standpoint of an ideal model which would meet the need for societal guidance and overcome the present limitations of our pluralistic, *ad hoc*, incremental form of planning and policy-making. One of the assumptions of this model is that government should be active with respect to anticipating the future and responsive to incipient conditions of social injustice or unrest.

Since some variation of centralized planning is inevitable in a complex society, a number of issues must be resolved if such planning is to become viable as well as socially responsible. How can the relationship between consensus and control be optimized? What is the suitable structure for centralized planning in America? What is the role of the planner in centrally planned change in a democratic society?

Optimizing Consensus and Control

The primary task in the development of planning theory is to identify structures and processes that can result in public decisions that are redistributive without creating dissension that threatens the viability of decision-making, or at the other extreme, diluting control over the resources necessary to resolve such issues through bargaining.

One can identify a variety of positions in current public debates about bases for consensus in public policy and social change.

1. In the absence of any clear-cut consensus regarding the direction for planned change, nothing should be done—in essence planners or policy-makers should await a public mandate. Such a position assures the continuation of the status quo and is a form of planning—"not to decide is to decide." This position is rejected as being an abdication of social responsibility even in the most narrow sense and one which even elected officials would find untenable.

2. Planners should rely exclusively on the political process for formulating and identifying the kinds of changes necessary. This position represents the dominant American tradition of incrementalism in public-policy formation which has been criticized as having inherent blindspots. Such a process prevents the formulation of large-scale policies or long-range goals, the absence of which may constitute substantial costs to the public.

3. A newer response is to work for alternative forms of institutions through a revolution in ideology or political structures. This response, like the first, is based on the assumption that only through participation of the body politic can any direction for social change be formulated. While such an approach may be necessary at a given point in time—indeed it may be necessary, at this time, to achieve new directions in American society—it does not avoid the dilemma between consensus and control. Once the new ideology or political institution is established, the dilemma will break out in that new context. One of the assumptions underlying this book is that any system will exhibit a tension between consensus and control because of the unavoidable heterogeneity of constituent interests.

4. A somewhat older response is to delegate a limited amount of power to some technical elite which is knowledgeable and free to formulate plans for societal guidance with periodic checks by a political process.

While this response is often associated with the model of centrally planned change reflected in Chapter 1, it is recognized to be in conflict with the American form of government, and fraught with the potential for totalitarianism.

5. The position that embraces the deliberations reflected in this book merges a political approach and a technocratic approach by injecting rational calculations into the political process.

This last position suggests that politics and planning are two parts of the same process. A primitive model can be drawn from the discussions in this book. When elaborated and empirically tested, the model may provide the basis for the technical calculations necessary for resolving the central issue of consensus and control. This model is inspired by choice theory in economics (reflected in the Phillips curve discussed in Chapter 2) in which a trade-off or negative relationship illustrates the effects of two conflicting values or objectives.

The model assumes that the relationship between the degree of control over resources needed to resolve a societal problem or change a structural variable and the amount of consensus in the body politic associated with the level of control proposed is quantifiable (see Figure 2, Graph A). The vertical axis represents the relative amount of public resources allocated to a given public program, for example, manpower training or remedial reading for children, or it may reflect the ability to make redistributive decisions, such as changing the tax structure or reallocating public services, as in the case of school desegregation. The horizontal axis is represented by a factor called consensus regarding such governmental intervention as reflected in elections or referenda or public opinion polls. The working of the simple model is reflected in the curve which shows the hypothesized variation in relationship between consensus and control—when control over resources is high, the degree of consensus is low, and as control lessens, consensus increases.

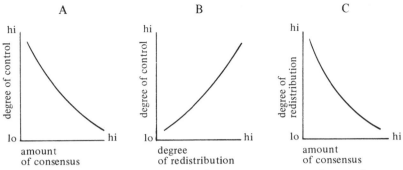

FIGURE 2. A model of the relationship between consensus and control.

This trade-off may be explained by certain other partial relationships in public decision-making. For example, it is hypothesized that control over resources will be positively correlated with the degree of redistribution of resources (Figure 2, Graph B). This proposition is based on the assumption that centralized control would have the authority to go against vested interests with respect to the expenditure of public monies to achieve specified objectives. However, redistribution is assumed to be negatively correlated with the degree of consensus, since the decision to change the pattern of public spending may generate resistance among groups, even though the results of such change may prove to be widely beneficial (Figure 2, Graph C). The conversion of defense spending to peacetime uses is a case in point. Thus these countervailing partial relationships, one negative and one positive, account for the over-all negative relationship hypothesized between consensus and control. At the present time there is no empirical evidence regarding the relative importance of these countervailing partial relationships, nor for that matter of the over-all relationship between consensus and control.

So far we have discussed only a partial model for public decision-making. What is lacking is a way of calculating the optimal point on the control-consensus curve. We need a point(s) of intersection based on other related variables. Such a point is

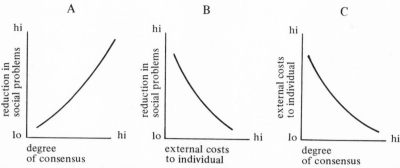

FIGURE 3. A model of the relationship between reduction in problems and consensus.

suggested by another relationship implied in our model of centrally planned change—that between consensus and the reduction in the level of social problems. It is hypothesized that the reduction of societal or public problems will be associated with an increase in consensus regarding the desirability of the actions taken (Figure 3, Graph A). This proposition is based on the assumption that there is widespread agreement about the undesirability of certain shared conditions, and that individuals so affected value public actions which eliminate or reduce the negative effects of those conditions.

This relationship also can be explained by certain partial relationships. For example, reduction in problem states can be assumed to be negatively correlated with "external costs" to the individual, that is, expenses incurred by the individual as the result of the behavior of others for which he cannot be compensated (Figure 3, Graph B). In turn, external costs to the individual can be assumed to be negatively related to consensus (Figure 3, Graph C). These negative partial relationships account for the over-all positive relationship between the reduction in problem states and amount of public consensus.

These two formulations can be put together into a tentative or hypothetical model for calculating the optimal relationship between control and consensus in any given proposal for centrally planned change. In Figure 4, the effect of different de-

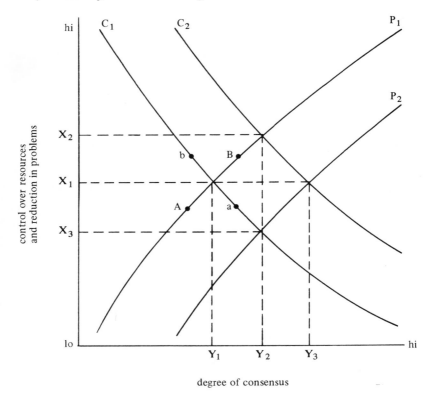

FIGURE 4. A model for calculating the optimal trade-off between consensus and control.

grees of control over resources on political consensus is reflected in the curve C_1. The effects of different levels of problem reduction on political consensus are reflected in the curve P_1. The intersection of C_1 and P_1 represents the optimal planning intervention in terms of control over problems, X_1, and consensus, Y_1. Any lower level of control, a, would increase consensus regarding intervention, but sow the seeds of dissension through a lower level of problem reduction, A. Any increase in control, b, would increase problem reduction, B, but result in a political stalemate over means and ends—the consensus over problem reduction would not be matched by a preference for the higher level of controls necessary.

Any hope of improving on this situation is represented by alternate curves C_2 and P_2. C_2 represents the situation in which the planner is able to devise a technology of intervention which is more politically acceptable, or in which a greater consensus has been reached about the desirability of governmental intervention. A higher degree of consensus is reached at every level of control exercised over problems. The introduction of this new technology includes a range of planning options which presumably varies along the curve P_1 from point X_1Y_1 to X_2Y_2. P_2 represents the situation in which the planner is able to increase public demand for problem solution reflected in higher levels of consensus for every degree of problem reduction. The potential for this increased demand introduces a range of planning options which presumably varies along the curve C_1 between points X_1Y_1 and X_3Y_2. However, it should be noted that in the absence of any change in type of control, the advantages of the greater demand result only in achieving higher levels of consensus with less effort, not greater problem reduction.

If both alternatives, C_2 and P_2, are possible, the planner's options are defined by the rectangle X_1Y_1, X_2Y_2, X_3Y_2, and X_1Y_3. The direction in which change is planned within that rectangle depends on the relative importance of each of the three variables involved—centralized control, problem reduction, and consensus. X_2Y_2 represents the point at which problem reduction is maximized; X_1Y_3, the point at which consensus is maximized.

Presumably the curves will differ depending on the nature of the problem being attacked. Problems may vary in the types of interventions to which they respond, and thus exhibit different C curves. Problems may vary in their responsiveness to intervention, or their favor with the public, thus exhibiting different P curves. In either event the model suggests that planners must concern themselves with more than just the treatment technology for a particular problem; *they must also consider the public ac-*

ceptability of alternative types of control represented by that technology and the public demand for problem reduction. In this process the planner need not treat control and consensus as fixed constraints. By introducing new control technologies, he may achieve higher levels of consent regarding intervention. By enlarging the consensus in the body politic regarding the need for intervention, he may achieve greater receptivity to control technology.

This attempt to depict the critical relationships between factors involved in centrally planned change has marked similarities to two other models of public policy analysis which have recently been formulated. One is called the "calculus of consent" and was developed by two economists, Buchanan and Tullock.[1] The other is based on a typology of policy actions developed by Lowi.[2] The convergence of these models holds promise for fruitful efforts to derive suitable and viable methodologies for centrally planned change.

For Buchanan and Tullock, the calculus of consent rests on the interrelationship between three factors: (1) the "expected external costs" to an individual of a collective or public decision, (2) the expected costs of making that decision, and (3) the "number of individuals required to take collective action," or the degree of centralized control in a group or collectivity. According to this model, the number of individuals required to take collective action is inversely related to the benefits which individuals in the group would expect to derive from such actions. If the number is small, the expectation of costs to other individuals is high. This relationship between external costs and collective decision-making is almost identical to our hypothesized negative relationship between control and consen-

[1] James M. Buchanan and Gordon Tullock, *The Calculus of Consent* (Ann Arbor, Mich.: University of Michigan Press, 1962).

[2] Theodore J. Lowi, "Decision-Making vs. Policy-Making: Toward an Antidote for Technocracy," *Public Administration Review*, 30 (May–June, 1970), pp. 314–325; and "Population Policies and the American Political System," in *Political Science in Population Studies*, eds. Richard L. Clinton, William S. Flash, R. Kenneth Godwin (Lexington, Mass.: Heath, 1972), pp. 25–53.

sus. In order to calculate the optimal level of consent, Buchanan and Tullock introduce the "costs of making collective decisions." They argue that as the number of persons required to make collective decisions increases (low control), the costs of making such decisions increases. Thus Buchanan and Tullock offer a model for centralized planning based on an almost identical trade-off between consensus and control, optimized on the basis of the costs of making collective decisions under differing degrees of control. In this latter respect the model differs from our own, even though the basic structure and substance of the models are quite similar.

The model developed by Theodore Lowi depicts the anticipated impact of various types of policies on political behavior. This model is not as elaborate nor as refined in terms of potentially measurable concepts. However, its similarities encourage continued work in this field. Lowi distinguishes between four types of policies: *distributive, constituent, regulatory*, and *redistributive*. Distributive policies tend to provide something for everybody and are the product of policy-making systems characterized by low centralized control over resources. Such policies tend to be relatively popular; they generate widespread consensus. On the other extreme are redistributive policies which tend to change the rules of the game or change the relationship between disparate elements in the body politic. They can be expected to generate lower levels of consensus and are likely to originate in more centralized structures of control. In between these two extremes are constituent policies which affect individuals by applying to the group as a whole but with a minimum of control (remoteness of coercion), and regulatory policies by which controls or coercion are more immediately applied but only on an individualized case-by-case basis, rather than to the group as a whole. Although not advocated by Lowi, presumably this typology of policy actions could be converted into a continuum which, when graphed against degrees of consensus reflected in accompanying political behavior, would result in a model almost identical to those discussed here.

The model we propose is suggestive at best. Considerable work is needed to find ways of quantifying or measuring the respective variables involved and to test the validity of the implied relationships. Any attempt to calculate the trade-off between consensus and control, it should be recognized, still does not touch the more basic problem of creating the necessary consensus to move society in new directions, to chart radically new goals, or to implement such goals in the face of opposition. The model does provide a more rational way of measuring the trade-off between the amount of structural change achieved and political consensus developed so that alternatives can be more clearly articulated and examined. Without such a technique to calculate the consequences of new directions, policy-makers are hesitant to venture into new directions.

The Future of Centralized Planning

We conclude this review of American experience with centrally planned change—albeit sketchy and incomplete—with the renewed conviction of its relevance for societal guidance. Little intentional use has been made of this form of planning, and what has occurred was often unduly confined in scope or time span or effort. This failing does not lie in ineffectiveness of centrally planned changes. Some rather dramatic outgrowths of centrally induced change have occurred on an unplanned or unintended basis—the full employment accompanying World War II, the creation of a racially segregated society, the balkanization of metropolitan areas. Nor are alternative models of planned intervention currently in vogue sufficient for societal guidance. We are forced to conclude that the model of centrally planned change, essentially as outlined at the beginning of this study, remains viable and necessary. The time frame, style of control, and scale may vary, but the basic conception remains valid.

The principal obstacle to the effective use of centrally

planned change stems not from a lack of validity, the absence of availability of appropriate technology, its lack of utility to the needs of society, nor its conflict with a democratic value system. The centralization of power is not inherently undemocratic, only the extent to which its use is accountable to the popular will. One has only to look at situations of national emergencies to find confirming examples.

The constraint on centrally planned change lies in the absence of consensus about social purpose written into American political institutions and raised to the level of folkway through our common national experience. Incrementalism is so embedded in the American way of life that it is difficult to imagine that it ever could be otherwise. The real issue is not the necessity or feasibility of centrally planned change, but how that sense of social purpose upon which any society depends can be achieved.

This review occurs at a time of turning away from nearly half a century of increasing centralization of power in American governance. There is a tendency to blame the ills of our society on the centralization of means, as though the treatment were the cause of the illness. The popular trend is to favor a dismantling of such forms of governance, to favor decentralization in a variety of forms, even the devolution of the state to the level of individual choice. *It is our conviction that such moves will not resolve the crucial problems of social equity and social justice which underlie our social ills.*

There are some signs of a public awareness that the way out lies not in dismantling the capacity for societal guidance but making it more effective and accountable. The principal mechanism for national planning in this country has been the executive branch of government whose ability to perpetrate centrally planned change has accumulated over the years by default and without popular design, as though to fill a vacuum. There is a growing demand that the ability to set national goals and launch large-scale plans be lodged in the legislative branch, which is more accountable to the popular will. Therein lies considerable hope for generating the consensus necessary for centrally planned change.

A second trend is the emerging energy crisis which may create, much as did the depression of the thirties and the two world wars, a sense of national interdependence and the necessity for making conscious choice of how our natural resources, both physical and human, might best be used.

We feel it is time for planners to reassert their faith in bold, rational decision-making about social purpose. Such a position is not in conflict with the recognition that collective ends must be built on popular consensus. We agree that politics and planning are part of the same process. To say that planners should be part of efforts to build consensus is not to reduce planning to politics, nor to manipulate the public will through planning. Machiavelli and Cellini must maintain their integrity in order to make their respective contributions to the commonweal.

PARTICIPANTS IN THE CONFERENCE ON CENTRALLY PLANNED CHANGE

Quail Roost, North Carolina. April 26–29, 1972

JIMMY ALGIE
National Institute for Social Work Training,
London, England

ROBERT L. BARRE
Washington, D.C.

DAVID DONNISON
Center for Environmental Studies, London, England

JOHN W. DYCKMAN
Department of City and Regional Planning,
University of California, Berkeley

GEORGE H. ESSER, JR.
The Ford Foundation

JACK C. FISHER
Center for Urban Studies, Wayne State University

JOEL FLEISHMAN
Institute of Policy Sciences and Public Affairs,
Duke University

BERNARD FRIEDEN
Harvard–Massachusetts Institute of Technology
Joint Center for Urban Studies

R. A. GORDON
Department of Economics, University of California, Berkeley

ARNOLD GURIN
Florence Heller Graduate School for Advanced Studies in
Social Welfare, Brandeis University

LEONARD HAUSMAN
Florence Heller Graduate School for Advanced Studies in
Social Welfare, Brandeis University

FREDERICK HAYES
New York City

A. R. ISSERLIS
Centre for Studies in Social Policy, London, England

ALFRED J. KAHN
School of Social Work, Columbia University

EDWARD J. LOGUE
Urban Development Corporation, State of New York

ROBERT R. MAYER
Department of City and Regional Planning,
University of North Carolina, Chapel Hill

DAVID MECHANIC
Department of Sociology, University of Wisconsin, Madison

ROBERT MORONEY
Department of City and Regional Planning,
University of North Carolina, Chapel Hill

ROBERT MORRIS
Florence Heller Graduate School for Advanced Studies in
Social Welfare, Brandeis University

WILLIAM NISKANEN
Office of Management and Budget, Executive Office
of the President

BENJAMIN PASAMANICK
Department of Mental Hygiene, State of New York

ANTHONY PASCAL
Rand Corporation

THOMAS PLAUT
National Institute of Mental Health

MARTIN REIN
Department of City and Regional Planning,
Massachusetts Institute of Technology

CHARLES RICHTER
Department of Economics, University of North Carolina,
Chapel Hill

ALLAN SCHICK
The Brookings Institution

ALVIN L. SCHORR
Graduate School of Social Work, New York University

MICHAEL STEGMAN
Department of City and Regional Planning,
University of North Carolina, Chapel Hill

JAMES L. SUNDQUIST
The Brookings Institution

MITCHELL SVIRIDOFF
The Ford Foundation

RICHARD WAKEFIELD
The Center for Studies of Metropolitan Problems,
National Institute of Mental Health

MELVIN M. WEBBER
Department of City and Regional Planning,
University of California, Berkeley

ALONZO S. YERBY
Department of Health Services Administration,
Harvard School of Public Health

INDEX

Adaptive planning: in city building, 19, 26; mentioned, 3
Administrative planning, 83
Advocacy planning, 134
Agricultural productivity, 22
Allocative planning, 81
Alonzo, William, 25
American cities: and individualism, 42; as open and experimental, 42
American Medical Association, 63, 66
American Psychiatric Association, 63
Antitrust legislation, 88
Appel, Dr. Kenneth, 63
Atomic Energy Commission, 153
Authority, 6, 9, 10, 13

Balance of payments, 48
Bargaining, 6, 177, 186
Benefit-cost analysis, 15, 84, 158, 162, 164. See also Planning technology
Britain: and authority for centrally planned change, 10; town planning in, 41; political leadership in, 187. See also London
Brookings Institution: as planning structure, 91; study of federal budget by, 170
Buchanan, James M., 216, 217
Budgetary process, 163, 164, 167, 175
Bureaucracies: private, 81; public, 81; independence of, 83; self-interest, 141; mentioned, 135, 136, 207

Cable television, 37
Calculus of Consent, 216

Cellini, 178, 196
Centralized control: technology of, 15; and problem reduction, 215; and redistributive policies, 217
Centralized planning: consensus about goals in, 5; and British welfare state, 10; American experiences in, 11; as incremental change, 16, 206; for community mental health, 67; requisites of, 88; formal structure of, 89; within decentralized framework, 134; with market mechanisms, 134; means of, 179; variations of, 205, 207; need for, 208; future of, 218; principal obstacle to, 219. See also Government intervention; Planning
—central dilemma of, 5, 7, 9, 88
—defined: as national in scope, 2; and control over resources, 3; and developmental planning, 3; participation in, by citizenry, 3
—model of, 207, 216, 218
Centrally unplanned change, 200
City building: implanned, 18, 20, 21; as atomistic decisions, 19, 40, 43; as unintended consequence, 22, 26; experimentation in, 40, 43. See also Urban growth policy; Urbanization
Civil rights: act, 1; legislation, 56; programs, 59
Clients and market, 8
Coleman, James, 171
Coleman Report, 169
Collective action, 43

Community mental health: movement, 65, 68; policy of, 69; failure
of, 77. *See also* Mental illness
Community mental health center, 61,
63, 66-76 *passim*
Community Mental Health Centers
Act, 1, 62, 68, 69, 70, 72
Comprehensive planning: defined, 86;
mechanisms for, 86, 91; mentioned,
5, 71, 186, 201
Congress, 13, 14, 15, 22, 23, 24, 25, 26
Congressional Reference Library, 92
Consensus: bases for, 6, 198, 209, 210,
211, 219, 220; building of, 6, 7, 8,
188; and parliamentary elections,
10; makers, 13; continuity of, 98,
99, 196, 201; and reduction in social
problems, 213, 214, 215
Consensus and control: inherent
conflict between, 6, 11; resolution of
conflict between, 8, 14, 200, 210,
220; optimal relationship of, 211,
212, 213, 215, 217; mentioned, 43,
199
Constitution writing, 134, 185, 186,
187
Consumers: expanding choice of, 8,
37, 44; of public services, 15; and
quality control, 39, 155; access to
market by, 139, 141; sovereignty of,
146; education, 151, 152; common
interests of, 207. *See also* Market;
Voucher/market systems
Contextual planning, 14
Contracts, 139, 208
Control: decentralized, 14; span of, 85;
centralized, 215, 216. *See also* Authority; Consensus and control
Coordinated Area Manpower Plan-
ning System, 170
Corporate planning, 5
Cost-effectiveness, 15, 158, 165. *See
also* Planning technology
Council of Economic Advisors, 46, 90
Cripps, Stafford, 187
Cultural pluralism, 29, 43
Cybernetic planning style, 21, 44

Decentralization: and centralized
planning, 7, 10, 11, 209; defined,
112, 113; of planning, 112, 134; and
common interest, 207; trends to-
ward, 219. *See also* Greater London
Council; Tiebout model; Yugo-
slavia
Decision-making: atomistic, 36; range
of options in, 37; techniques of, 161;
expected costs of, 216
Delivery of public services, 33, 72, 77.
See also Public goods and services
Demonstration programs, 3
Denmark, 41
Department of Defense, 13, 165, 166,
167
Department of Health, Education,
and Welfare, 166, 167
Department of Housing and Urban
Development, 83
Direct cash transfers, 145
Disjointed incrementalism, 3, 9. *See
also* Incrementalism
Distribution of resources, 208, 212
Dror, Yehezkel, 5, 10, 134, 185

Economic growth, 48
Economic opportunity, 59
Education: policies for, 35; equal op-
portunity in, 147; evaluation of,
169. *See also* Schools
Elitism, 201, 210
Eminent domain, 154
Employment: full, 45, 58, 218; goal of,
46, 47; policy of, 47, 48, 50; and
price stability, 48. *See also* Unemployment
Employment Act of 1946, 45, 46
Employment service: federal-state, 54
Equality: of economic opportunity,
60; as public good, 137; among
races, 201. *See also* Race
Equity, 155
Evaluation: examples of, 162, 169,
170, 171; raises methodological disputes, 171; underlying logic of, 172;
as threat to politicians, 175, 199;

time pressure on, 175; of first principles, 198, 199, 200; of multiple goals, 198; of public policy, 199; of market mechanisms, 208. *See also* Planning technology

Externalities, 8, 18, 28, 34, 43, 208. *See also* Market

Extra-market mechanisms, 145

Federal Deposit Insurance Corporation, 180
Federal government: as banker, 34; new roles of, 34, 35. *See also* Government
Federal Housing Administration, 22, 176, 180
Federal manpower programs: evaluation of, 170. *See also* Employment; Evaluation
Federal military and space expenditures, 24
Feld, S., 74
Fiscal and monetary controls, 15, 158
Food and Drug Administration, 90
Forecasting, 15, 158
Forrester, Jay, 175
Frictional unemployment, 52, 54, 55. *See also* Unemployment
Friedmann, John, 7

General Accounting Office, 92
General purpose legislation, 13
Glazer, Nathan, 29
Gordon, Robert A., 18
Government: planning in, 5, 80, 190; territorially defined, 31, 32; private, 31, 36; national, 33, 36; regulation in, 80, 81; structures for planning, 92; contrasts in, 141; activities of, 179, 180, 181; lower level of, 179; intervention by, 182-185 *passim,* 189, 191, 192, 193. *See also* Local government; Public goods and services
Great Society, 88, 163, 165, 166
Greater London Council, 127, 128, 132. *See also* Decentralization

Guided planning methods, 85
Gurin, G., 74

Health Services Administration, 91
High-scale society, 39, 43
Highway construction program, 23
Human services, 34, 35

Immigration, 22
Incentives, 85, 165, 177, 208
Income: tax provisions, 23; distribution of, 145, 151; guarantees, 146; transfer, 146; equalization of, 147
Incrementalism: defined, 4; criticized, 5; and technology, 93, 163, 167, 174; and scale of intervention, 202, 203, 207, 210; and pluralism, 209; mentioned, 15, 159, 187, 201, 219. *See also* Marginalism; Scale of intervention
Indifference curves, 50
Industry: moves to suburbs, 60
Inequality, racial, 194
Inflation, 46, 48, 49, 50, 54, 57, 58
Inner city, 149
Innovation, 94, 177
Innovative planning, 3, 87
Institute for Research on Poverty, University of Wisconsin, 91
Institutional change, 180, 182, 210
Integration: of national society, 36
Interest-based communities, 31, 34
Interest group liberalism, 4
Interest groups: competition among, 81, 82, 83, 160; aggregating interests of, 134
Interstate Commerce Commission, 90
Intervention. *See* Government intervention
Intervention theory, 172

Job discrimination, 56
Job opportunities, 170
Johnson, President Lyndon B., 67
Johnson administration, 46
Joint Commission on Mental Illness and Health, 63, 64, 74

Joint Economic Committee, 171
Joint Information Service, 73
Judiciary, 8

Kennedy, President John F., 64, 65
Kennedy administration, 46
Kuhn, Thomas S., 203

Labor: turnover, 52; demand for, 59
Labor force: age-sex composition of,
    47, 50, 57; changing age-sex com-
    position of, 47; immobility of, 53.
    See also Employment
Labor market: segmented, 51, 52, 56
Laissez-faire, 39, 43, 80
Land Grant College Act, 88
Lead time, 98
Learning from experience, 176, 192,
    203
Legislature: as consensus-makers, 13;
    as planner, 219
Local control, 14
Local government: intervention, 33;
    autonomy of, 35; declining roles for,
    36. *See also* Government
London, 126, 127, 128
Lowi, T. J., 4, 12, 216, 217
Lowrey, Ira S., 149

Machiavelli, 178, 196
Management, 93, 174, 177
Manpower: programs, 53, 54, 56, 60;
    policy, 57, 58, 59; training, 135
Manpower Development and Train-
    ing Act, 1
Marginalism: advantages of, 190, 191;
    disadvantages of, 193, 194; men-
    tioned, 19, 183, 195, 201. *See also*
    Incrementalism; Scale of interven-
    tion
Market: and delivery of public goods,
    7, 8, 135, 138, 156, 179, 207; regula-
    tion of, 8, 151; as basis of planning,
    9, 12, 155, 156, 157, 179, 207;
    mechanisms of, 9, 14, 135, 136, 147,
    152, 153, 154; and consumer choice,
    15, 141; and city building, 26; pro-

ducers in, 83; and social goals, 136,
    156; and structural change, 147;
    barriers to open, 149; breakdown
    of, 149. *See also* Consumers;
    Voucher/market system
Mass society, 30
McNamara, Rae, 18
Medicaid, 140, 174
Medical care: cost of, 144; increased
    demand and supply of, 145
Medicare, 1
Megapolicies, 3, 5
Mental health. *See* Community mental
    health
Mental Health Study Act of 1955, 63
Mental illness: and hospitalization, 62,
    64, 75, 76; and community model,
    75; and medical model, 75, 76
Merit goods (wants), 8, 43
Meta-planning, 134, 185
Metropolitan areas, 24, 149, 184, 203,
    218
Metropolitan development corpora-
    tion, 7
Migration, 22, 34
Military research and development, 25
Minority groups, 4, 6, 7, 19, 27, 55, 58
Mobility, 30, 35
Model Cities, 1, 135, 170, 171
Monetary controls, 158
Mosteller, Fredrich, 171
Moynihan, Daniel P., 29, 171, 176

*Nader Report on Community Mental
    Health Centers*, 77
National Aeronautics and Space Ad-
    ministration, 153
National Institute of Mental Health,
    62, 64, 65, 67, 73, 83, 91
National Mental Health Act of 1963,
    69
Natural monopolies, 136
Negotiation, 6, 134, 177
Netherlands, 41
New Deal, 88
New-town movement, 18, 22, 41

Nixon administration, 46
Norris, Linda, 18

Office of Management and Budget, 92
Office of Research and Development, 180

Pacific Railway Act, 88
Parliamentary election, 10
Pasamanick, Benjamin, 18
Perry, George, 47
Phillips, A. W., 48
Phillips curve, 48, 49, 50, 53, 54, 57
Planners: as mediators, 7; above special interests, 12; and political context, 99; as critics of value system, 201. *See also* Planning
Planning: and unintended consequences, 22, 197, 200, 203; and incentives, 38; contextual, 44; rationality of, 78, 89, 160; minimalist approach to, 82; as thinking, 86, 195, 206; and nonplanning, 88; and Congress, 29, 219; time dimension to, 96, 97, 98, 175, 194, 218; as constitution writing, 185, 186, 187; as climate setting, 187; as an art, 188; public mandate for, 210
—belief systems (first principles), 192, 193, 198, 199, 200, 206
—as choice expansion, 37, 38, 39, 44
—and governmental activities, 88, 179, 180, 181
—as learning, 20, 44, 87, 192, 195, 203
—national, 17, 24, 74, 89
—as political process, 159, 160, 188, 211
—as relating systems, programs, 44, 79, 85, 181, 186, 202
—and social change, 93, 181, 183, 192
—structures for, 12, 14, 84, 90, 91, 92, 93
—types of, 80, 81, 85, 86, 87, 88, 93, 94
Planning-programming-budgeting (PPB), 84, 162-177 *passim. See also* Planning technology

Planning technology: types of, 15, 160, 161, 162; purpose of, 158, 159; limitations of, 173-177 *passim*
Plaut, Thomas, 18
Pluralism: and planning, 4, 6, 9, 15, 209; and city building, 19, 27, 29, 30, 37, 39, 44; and technology, 177
Policies: types of, 216, 217
Political leadership, 187, 201
Postindustrial city, 27, 28, 42
President's Commission on School Finance, 169
Price stability, 47, 48. *See also* Inflation
Program Evaluation and Review Technique, 84
Public goods and services: defined, 8, 136, 139, 140; provision for, by government, 14, 15, 137, 138, 142, 143, 148, 155; variety of, 37; examples of, 136, 137, 138; mentioned, 43, 141, 142, 208. *See also* Market; Voucher/market system
Public housing, 24, 170
Public interest, 6

Race: segregation, 23, 218; integration, 147; discrimination, 148, 194; inequality, 197; equality, 201
Rational planning, 78, 89, 160. *See also* Planning
Redistributive functions, 134, 146, 183
Reduction in problem states, 213
Regulatory functions, 15, 158, 177
Regulatory planning, 80, 81, 94
Resource allocation, 82, 83

Scale of intervention: and consensus, 94, 95; and size of problem, 96, 202, 207; massive, 189, 190, 194, 206; and unintended consequences, 203; mentioned, 182, 218. *See also* Incrementalism; Marginalism
Scale of system, 33, 44
Schools: public, 142, 147, 152; private, 148. *See also* Education

Securities and Exchange Commission, 90

Serrano v. *Priest*, 35

Social Security Administration, 13, 83, 84, 91

Special interest groups, 4, 12

Stanford Achievement Test, 172

Stegman, Michael A., 149

Sternlieb, George, 149

Structural unemployment, 46, 52-59 *passim. See also* Employment

Suboptimization, 5

Suburbanization, 23, 24

Supreme Court decisions, 1

Sweden, 41

Technology. *See* Planning technology

Tiebout, Charles, 114

Tiebout model, 111, 114-119 *passim*, 132. *See also* Decentralization

Time dimension. *See* Planning

Tito, Marshal, 11

Tullock, Gordon, 216, 217

Unemployment: rate of, 46, 47, 58, 59, 170; structural, 46, 52-59 *passim;* and aggregate demand, 51; frictional, 51-58 *passim;* ratio of job vacancies to, 51; seasonal, 55, 56; ghetto, 59; and inflation, 60. *See also* Employment; Inflation

Urban crescent (South), 24

Urban growth policy, 20, 21, 24, 25, 26, 40, 41. *See also* City building

Urban guidance systems, 20, 21

Urban Institute, 91

Urban renewal, 23, 41, 170, 196

Urban spatial structure, 40

Urbanization: unintended, 22, 23, 24, 26, 28, 39, 43; of West Coast, 25; national, 27, 31. *See also* City building

Veroff, J., 74

Voucher/market systems: defined, 138; examples of, 138, 139, 144, 151; benefits of, 139, 140, 141; criticisms of, 141-149 *passim;* as necessary correctives, 142, 143, 150, 151; and level of consumption, 146; and income distribution, 147; and structural change, 148; differentials, 148; experience of, in European countries, 150; mentioned, 136, 179. *See also* Consumers; Market

Wage and price controls, 47

Wage Price Control Boards, 90

Wagner Act, 180

War on Poverty, 1, 135

Webber, Melvin M., 17

Welfare, 48, 50

Work incentive program, 170

Workmen's protective laws, 88

Yugoslavia, 9, 10, 11, 16, 111, 119-126 *passim*, 132. *See also* Decentralization